5 Point SINGING SYSTEM
For Popular Music Styles

Angela Kelman

5 Point SINGING SYSTEM
For Popular Music Styles

To access the video tutorials see page 115

"A great teacher is one who realizes

that he himself is also a student

and whose goal is not to dictate the answers,

but to stimulate his students creativity enough

so that they go out

and find the answers themselves."

Herbie Hancock

DEDICATION

To my students - past, present and future.

It is you who teach me and I am ever so grateful.

To see you blossom and find your own voice

once enlightened

has been and continues to be a joyous

and rewarding experience.

Angela Kelman

Cover Photo by Lee Halliday
Styling by Jake Leiske
Make Up by Sonia Leal-Serafim (theyrep.com)

TESTIMONIALS

"One night at about 2am after copious amounts of cocktails, Angela Kelman, decided to give me a vocal lesson and run me through her 5 Point Singing System Diagnoses. She was impressed with my vocal abilities, breathing, range, pitch and projection and deemed me a rock star! In all honesty, Angela understands the nuances of the human voice and has developed an amazing system to guide each and every one of us to understanding our own voices. I have watched Angela in action on many occasions as well as had the opportunity to work with her. She is a consummate pro and in my opinion , **she is a rock star!"**

Mike Reno, Lead Singer **"Loverboy"**

"As a mature singer-songwriter, I had developed many bad habits that other vocal coaches had never successfully addressed. Everything I have learned from Angela's manual about singing, I have been able to incorporate into my song-writing as well. The additional information on microphone techniques and studio recording have been extremely helpful."

Catherine Bowers

"You don't have to be Celine Dion to be a diva! I have been able to find my voice and let my inner star shine by using Angela's 5 Point Singing System. I was a bit intimidated at the thought of voice training as I had never had formal music training, but I have learnt so much about my voice and gained confidence in this easy to use and easy to understand system. Most of all I have had fun! I could not recommend it highly enough."

Alyson Jones

"If something in my voice doesn't sound or feel right, I simply have to check in with my 5 point system and very quickly discover what I need to do to rectify it, and strangely enough, when I hear others sing, it becomes obvious which one of their 5 points have "broken down". It is ridiculous how simple it is when it is taught to you in such a basic and easy to follow manner. Angela's approach to coaching is hands on, experiential and NOT highly technical which makes it easy and fun for anyone to learn how to sing. Above all, Angela has walked the journey, knows how to get it done, and encourages others to follow suit."

Sue-Ann MacCara

5 Point SINGING SYSTEM
For Popular Music Styles
© 2016 by Angela Kelman

ISBN 978-0-9864733-6-4

All rights reserved. No part of this book may be used or reproduced in any manner whatsoever without the written permission of the publisher. Full distribution rights go to both the publisher and the author.

For more information please write to the publisher at:

Angela Kelman
Polyester Music Productions
infopolyestermusicproductions@gmail.com

www.angelakelman.com
5PointSingingSystem.com

Foreword

My dearest soul sister Angela, whom I love and respect more than words can say,

I'm writing your foreword in the form of a letter to you *(did I just hear you say, "ooooh boy"?)*. After reading the **'how to's"** of writing a proper foreword, I decided to ditch the directions and do something completely different. I know you're going to clutch your pearls and gasp just a bit, but hey, I'm following the fresh innovative nature of your book. Talking to you about anything is always the easiest, so here goes.

I look back at our lives so far and feel like there have been several of them. From every one of those lives we take the knowledge, education, experiences and personalities (those existing in our heads and those we've met along the way) on to the next portion of the show. We just keep gathering – and living. People like you with the Capricorn, steel-trap, compartmentalizing, date-stamping type brains make brilliant writers. All knowledge just sticks up there. I still call you to clarify details of stories concerning **MY OWN** family. *"Hey Ange, was it Aunt Cheryl who ran off with the hairy circus guy?" "No, that was your Aunt Verl."* You always know. It's amazing. The name *"Trivia Tracey"* did not fall on your shoulders par accident!

I think about the *"gathering"* you've done – from your formal vocal education in L.A. at MI to the truly uncountable gigs; from lounges to saloons, and bars to bar mitzvahs; from backyard bbqs to stadiums of people singing along to the words of the songs you've written. You've put a lot of miles on those vocal cords.

I can't help but elaborate on the lifespan of experiences that we gathered together during our years of being Jake and Angela of Farmer's Daughter. My lord! 270 days of the year on the road, 4 CDs *(2 which achieved gold status),* 49 major award nominations, 12 charting music videos, as well as tours across Canada, Germany, Holland, France, and the U.S. Remember the military treks that took us to Egypt, Israel, Bosnia, Africa, and Alert? *(I know-that's a lot of info. I got bored one day and Google stalked us…* **WOW** *learned that all on the* **WWW.** *no wonder we were so tired!!).*

The next phase: **"teaching."** Both of us found it a natural transition to share what we learned with students who were wanting more out of their singing experience. It cracks me up when I hear people say, "Those who cannot do, teach." Maybe it should be, "Those who cannot do, teach poorly." Connection to the **"doing"** is what makes you a great teacher, Ange. It's one thing to have a gift – something you just wake up and do without thinking twice. It's quite another to be able to figure out what's going on from a technical standpoint and explain it so clearly that a beginner can understand! I mean, even as a vocal coach myself there were **"a-ha"** moments reading your book – moments when I thought, what a great way to explain that. Being able to isolate and express what it should feel like makes you a bit of a miracle worker. I've heard with my own ears some of your success stories. This system really works!

Foreword *Continued*

I've stood beside you on stage more times than I can count. We've experienced everything that performance scenarios could throw at us: sound mishaps, natural disasters, laughing fits, crying fits, even running off stage to be sick and running back out with a big smile to finish the show. The whole enchilada! You are without a doubt one of the most dynamic singers/communicators I know. You have mastered your craft, and the fact that you've found a way to pass your secrets *(well, secrets no longer)* along with such a fresh spin is such good luck for anyone reading this book. I myself would have left a **POINT** or two out, you know, like a recipe that you pass along with the missing ingredient so it doesn't turn out perfectly, but that's me *(sly smile)!*

At the end of all this, Ange, I hope you understand the full importance of this singing system you've created. Singing can be the most joyful experience in the world or the most frustrating for the singer *(AND those having to listen!).* You've developed, refined and tested a highly successful method of becoming the master of your vocal cords – it's your own beautiful, freshly spun path of gaining access to the illusive voice!

So, here's to one more adventure sister. Can't wait to see what's next!

Love, love, love,

Jake   *"The Redhead in Farmer's Daughter"*

Introduction

I've known since I was 5 years old that I wanted to be a singer when I grew up. I'm not quite sure what put that idea into my head, but by the time I saw the first episode of *The Partridge Family* on television I was on a mission. I am a child of the 70s, an era of great music and television that became an intrinsic part of who I am as a person and as a singer/entertainer. For the next twenty years of my life, I followed my dream and honed my skills through the ever so effective *"school of hard knocks,"* performing in lounges and bars, recording commercial jingles in the studio and both performing on and hosting numerous television music specials.

In 1989, I decided it might be time to gain some musical insight into what I was doing by enrolling in the vocal program at the Musicians Institute in Hollywood, California. Being a realist and understanding that sometimes in the music business you may need *"something to fall back on,"* I thought that MI's vocal program would give me a better understanding of how to enhance my own vocal abilities as well as help me create a method by which to teach others to reach their vocal potential. It turned out to be a wonderful experience that helped me identify the things I was doing correctly vocally as well as insight for fixing my vocal challenges.

Well, after 20 more years of travelling the world with an award winning recording act, *"Farmer's Daughter,"* releasing my latin flavoured solo cd's *"Café Brasilia"* and *"Casa Do Samba,"* performing with my dream band, **"The Polyester Philharmonic,"** creating a series of Children's **"Sing-A-Long" Books,** being a mother, wife, and vocal coach, here is that method which I am ready to share with you.

"Utilizing Angela Kelman's **5 Point Singing System,** *in just a few months, I have gone from having my demos rejected because of the quality of the vocals to having one of my original songs* (with my vocal) *accepted by an international song publisher for placement"....*
Catherine Bowers, singer-songwriter

If you have this book in your hand, you are searching for some insight on how to become a better singer. In my **5 Point Singing System** vocal coaching program, I have simplified the instruction into **5 Points** with relatable terminology and guidance to validate what you are doing correctly and diagnose your vocal challenges. I walk you through the **5 Points** *(Breathing, Diaphragm Support, Placement/Resonance, Vocal Path, and Vowel Modification)* with easy-to-understand descriptions of what your body should feel like when singing, along with exercises for better awareness of how to improve upon each Point. There is also bonus material that I wanted to include to help you become the best performer you can in a short amount of time because becoming sensational is easily attainable with a little knowledge and guidance.

Introduction *Continued*

"Ha!! OMG I did it, Angela. I really, really, really did. I sang on stage in front of people, followed all your Points and it was fun, and I was relaxed...so cool...Yay! Thank you for believing in me and giving me the guidance I needed to get my voice heard. Wow, wow, wow...You are the best, Angela!"...
Elizabeth Wooding on overcoming her performance anxiety by working her way through the 5 Point Singing System which gave her confidence to just SING and enjoy it.

In all the years I have been teaching and developing my vocal program, nothing has excited me *(or moved me to tears)* more than seeing/hearing a student blossom once they understand the 5 Point Singing System. I have had students *(who I was sure were one step from being tone deaf)* who embraced the program, did the homework and reaped the rewards of finally being able to sing a melody with great pitch and confidence. I am a firm believer that everyone can become a better singer, and the 5 Point Singing System has proven that time and time again in my vocal studio with both beginners and professionals alike.

Learning to sing effortlessly with confidence should be a journey that is both fun and enlightening. It has been my dream to share everything I have learned about singing and performance with as many people as possible. My desire is to be able to help you discover the bliss and often euphoric feeling of singing and connecting emotionally with music which is, in my opinion, as great as the feeling of falling in love.

Happy Singing!

Angela

CONTENTS

15
POINT - 1
BREATHING

Chest Breathers – Expand Your Tank! 17
Correct Movement Of The Breath 17
Regulating The Breath 18
Breathing Rhythm 18
"Mapping Out" Lyrics 19

BREATHING EXERCISES

Breathing Exercise 1 20
Book On Tummy Exercise

Breathing Exercise 2 22
Hand On Tummy Exercise

Open Throat Breathing Exercise 23
Puppy Pant Exercise 23

TROUBLESHOOTING

Be Aware of Over Breathing 24
Heads Up For "Backwards Breathing" 24
"H Seepage" 25
"The Stacker" 25
"The Squeezer" 25
"The Hourglass Breather" 26
"The Faker" 26

AIR EXCHANGE 26

27
POINT - 2
DIAPHRAGM SUPPORT

Low-Range Notes 29
Mid-Range and Upper-Mid-Range Notes... 30
High-Range Notes 31
High-Range / Powerful Notes 32

Mapping Out Your Diaphragm Support........ 33

Diaphragm Exercise 1 34
Motor Boat Lips

Diaphragm Exericise 2 34
"1-2-3-4-5-4-3-2-1-5-1 Exercise

Diaphragm Exercise 3 34
"Huh Huh" Exercise

Diaphragm Exercise 4 35
The 1-5 Exercise on "Huh" and "Hee"

AIR TO TONE RATIO 35

37
POINT - 3
PLACEMENT / RESONANCE

Chest Placement 39
Full Voice/Speaking Tonality Placement 39
Diva/Rockstar Placement 40
Mask Area Placement 41
Supermask Area Placement 42

45
POINT - 4
VOCAL PATH

The "AH" Vocal Path 47

The "EE" Vocal Path 47

Vocal Path Exercise 1
"AH to EE" 48

The "OO" Vocal Path 49

Vocal Path Exercise 2
"AH to EE to OO" 50

WORKING IN THE DEGREES OF THE VOCAL PATH 50

53
POINT - 5
VOWEL MODIFICATION

The "A" Vowel Sounds 56

Vowel Modification Exercise 1
"Short A" to "AH" 56

The "E" Vowel Sounds 57

Vowel Modification Exercise 2
"EE" to "EH" 57

The "I" Vowel Sounds 58

Vowel Exercise 3
"I-EE" to "AH-y" 58

The "O" Vowel Sound 59

The "U" Vowel Sound 59

Summary 60
Enough About Vowels -
What About Consonants? 60

Consonants and Music Style 60

VIBRATO-O-O-O-O-O 63
Vibrato and Diaphragm Support 63
Vibrato And Vocal Cords 63

Vibrato Exercise 1
Half-Step Oscillation 64

Examples of Vibrato 65
Slow and Wide Vibrato 65
Fast and Narrow Vibrato 66
Vibrato Control 66
Don't Get Frustrated - My Vibrato Story 68

71
BONUS CHAPTERS
LIVE & STAGE PERFOMANCE

MAPPING OUT YOUR LYRICS REVISITED
Breathmarks 71
Diaphragm Support 71
Trills 72
Colour Words 72
Modifying Or Opening Vowels 72
Clipping Words 73
Notating Direction Of The Melody 73
Train Your Brain 73
Mapping Out - Exercise 1 73

MICROPHONE TECHNIQUE FOR LIVE PERFORMANCE
Low-Range 75
(Chest Voice Placement)

Mid-Range 75
(Full Voice/Speaking Tonality Placement)

Upper-Mid-Range 76
(Diva/Rockstar Placement)

Higher And Lighter Range 76
(Mask Area Placement)

Higher Range With Power 76
(Supermask Placement)

Microphone Positioning 77
Finding The Right Microphone 78

STAGE PERFORMANCE TIPS
Microphone Stands 81
Songs, Keys and Tempos 81
Composing A Set List 82
Connecting With Your Audience 82
R.E.S.P.E.C.T. On Stage 84
Stage Attire 84

87
BONUS CHAPTERS
FASHION, STUDIO, BGs & HEALTH

JAKE'S FASHION AND STYLE PHILOSOPHY 87
Guest Chapter by Jake Leiske

STUDIO SINGING
Studio Vocabulary 91
Studio Etiquette - Gear 92
Getting What You Want In Your Mix ... 93
Studio Microphone Technique 93
Troubleshooting Pitch Problems 93
Hydrate, Hydrate, Hydrate! 94

BACK-UP SINGING 101
The Role Of A "BG" Singer
Live Performance 97

Movement Of The "BG" Singer
Live Performance 99

"BG" Singing In The Studio 99

MAINTAINING A HEALTY VOICE
Water, Water, Water! 103
Exercise 103
Smoke, Smoke, Hack, Hack, Choke! ... 103
Feeling Under The Weather 103
Laughing 104

106
GLOSSARY

Glossary 106
Notes 107
About The Author 113

Acknowledgements 114
Additional Products by Angela Kelman 115

POINT - 1
BREATHING

POINT 1 - BREATHING

Breathing is life: without it, one cannot survive. The life of a song also depends on the art of breathing to enable the performer to reach out and touch their audience. For a singer, learning to breathe purposefully and correctly is the secret to enabling great power, pitch and tone. The projection of emotion to a listener and the ability to infuse a song with stylistic nuances are all based on good breath control. The sound of the breath can be sensual or soothing, or it can create angst or urgency in the performance of a song.
Mastering the breath is a singer's most powerful tool. Let's get started with learning to breathe correctly.

Chest Breathers - Expand Your Tank!

Have you ever watched a baby breathe while they are sleeping? You will notice that their tummy and chest rise and fall effortlessly with each breath. Somewhere along our journey of life we forget how to correctly maintain this very basic human mechanism. We have become a society of shallow chest breathers.
We are usually in such a hurry that we forget to breathe deeply and take in as much of that delicious oxygen as our midsection and chest combined, or what I like to call our "tank," can hold. As a singer, the first thing I want you to become aware of is how you breathe naturally. Concentrate on breathing from the belly button up, not just the chest up, making your body aware of the capacity of your air tank.

Correct Movement Of The Breath

The movement of the breath into your body is as important as getting the breath in. The proper way to take a singer's breath is to imagine sucking air in through a tube into your mouth. While the air is coming into your body, your tummy should be expanding as if filling up a balloon from your bellybutton upward. *(This is a bit of a challenge for those of us who have been told to keep our stomach sucked in all our lives. Let your inner beer belly hang out, everyone – at least until you get the hang of taking a singer's breath correctly.)*
Don't worry – you won't always have to think of it as sucking in through a tube. We'd have a lot of funny looking singers if everyone took each breath this way. This visual just makes it easier to understand at the beginning. So, remember "air in/tummy out" to fill up the tank. The direction that your tummy moves when breathing in and learning to regulate the amount of air you take in with each individual breath are the secrets to having great pitch and power.

Regulating The Breath

In the performance of a song, each phrase will vary in length. It is important that you learn to regulate your breathing for each individual line, or phrase, of a song. You don't want to take in a maximum size breath when you only have a 4-word phrase to sing. Having too much leftover, or residual air, at the end of a phrase will cause problems as you will read later in this chapter. For example, when performing a song, each new breath may require varying degrees of the capacity of your air tank to be used. A phrase or line of a song with 4 or 5 words in your lower range may only need **30%** of the total air capacity in your tank, while another phrase that has 10 words, is in a higher range, and needs power to project may need **100%** of the total air capacity in your tank. Where the notes in a song sit in your range, how much air you let escape around your tone for emotional effects, how much power you want to sing a phrase with and the length of a phrase are all determining factors as to how much air, or tank capacity, you need to take in between breathing points.

Learning to identify and regulate the amount of air needed for each phrase will rapidly become second nature. The song will always give you clues as to what it needs from you, breathing-wise, with each phrase. You will understand this more when we talk about "mapping out" a song later in this and subsequent chapters.

Breathing Rhythm

Every song has a different phrasing pattern. Very quickly, you will start getting a feel for where the breathing points in the song naturally occur, making the delivery of the song seem effortless. This is called "the breathing rhythm" and is unique to every song. Every time you learn a new song, it is imperative to mark on the lyric sheet where you will be breathing. By doing this, you are also identifying phrases, which are the lines of lyrics between each breath mark.

"Mapping Out" Lyrics – Step 1

Breathmarks

As mentioned earlier, each time you are learning a new song, it is important to "map out" your lyrics by marking each space where you should take a breath. Use a check mark, a star, a slash, a heart – whatever will become your personal symbol to remind you to BREATHE at this particular point in the song. This action will help create the unique "breathing rhythm" of each song. I guarantee you that **90%** of the challenges you will encounter in the delivery of your song will be related to incorrect or missed breaths. Sometimes phrases will be shorter between breaths indicating that you may only need to take in a smaller capacity breath, say **30%.** Conversely, you may notice that there are some really long phrases with no place to breathe indicating that you will need to take in a larger capacity breath, say **90%**, in order to have enough air to get through the entire phrase and to enable your diaphragm support. As indicated later in this chapter, it is very important to let go of any residual air before taking in a new breath. In *Figure 1* below I have used the chorus of a famous **Motown** song **Ain't No Mountain High Enough** as an example of what a "mapped out" lyric sheet with breathmarks looks like. I have also put the suggested use of your air tank capacity in parenthesis.

Figure 1

    (√ = **breathe**)

√'Cause Baby there *(3-word phrase – 30% tank capacity)*

√Ain't no mountain high enough *(upper-mid-range, 5 words – 60% tank capacity)*

√Ain't no valley low enough *(upper-mid-range, 5 words - 60% capacity)*

√Ain't no river wide enough *(upper-mid-range, 5 words, diaphragm "pull" to land on the note for "river" – 70% capacity)*

√To keep me from gettin' to you Babe *(mid-range, less diaphragm support needed, 8 words – 50% capacity)*

Breathing Exercises

Breathing Exercise 1- Book On Tummy Exercise

Whether you are a beginner or an experienced singer, this exercise will teach or remind you of the proper movement of the air in/tummy out principal. This exercise is perfect for understanding the movement of the singer's breath, when following the directions below.

a) Lie on your back with a heavy book on your tummy, just below the junction of your ribs and over your belly button.

Breathing Exercise 1-a

b) Through your mouth, suck in a breath while counting to 4 in your head, making the book rise up as high as possible by filling up your tank within the 4 counts.

Breathing Exercise 1-b

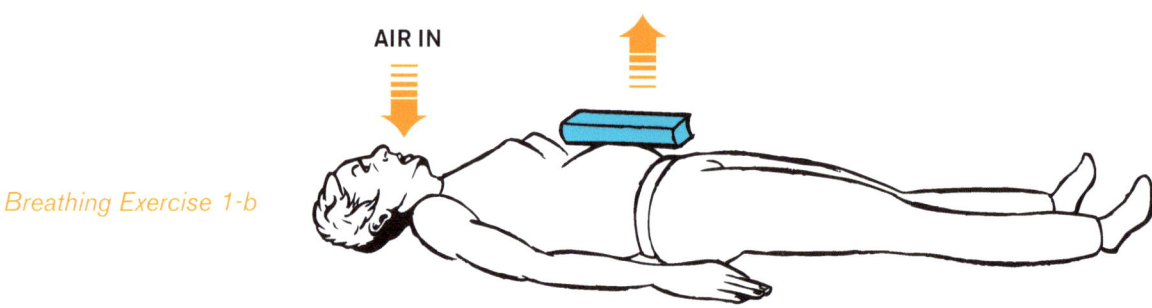

c) Now release the air through your mouth making an elongated "huh" sound on one note.

Let the book drop towards your backbone in a controlled manner, letting out all your air by the time you hit the 4 count in your head. This will be a fairly quick release of the breath. This is the proper movement for a singer's breath. Once again, think as if your tummy were a balloon. As you suck air into it *(inhaling)*, it fills up and rounds out . As you release the air *(exhaling)*, it becomes flat.

Breathing Exercise 1-c

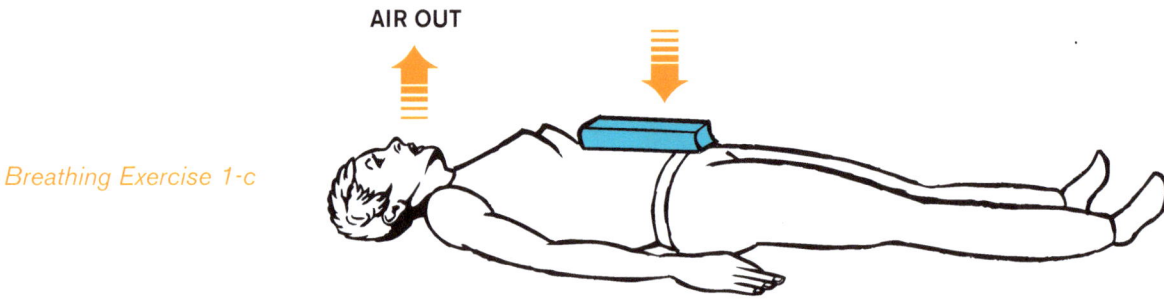

d)   Repeat the exercise a couple of times with the 4 count breath in to fill up your tank and the 4 count breath out on "huh," always being aware of the controlled exhalation.

e)   Repeat a 4 count breath in and a 6 count breath out on "huh," depleting all your air and flattening out your tummy by the "6" count. You are now manipulating your diaphragm muscle to resist the urge to just let your tummy fall quickly back towards the backbone and are learning to regulate the exhalation, or phrase, just as if you were singing it in the context of a song.

f)   Repeat a 4 count breath in and an 8 count breath out on "huh," depleting all your air and flattening out your tummy by the "8" count. Again, the controlled, elongated exhalation will allow you to achieve the desired effect.

g)   Finally, take a 4 count breath in and a 10 count breath out on "huh," depleting all your air and flattening out your tummy by the "10" count using control to lengthen the exhalation.
The inhalation will remain a 4 count as breathing "in" is, more often than not, in a smaller space of time in a song. This practice in balancing inhalation with differing lengths of exhalation is helping you create a sense of phrasing which you will eventually use in the performance of a song as the notes "float out" on the breath.

Refer to video tutorial **"Singer's Breath"**

Breathing Exercise 2

Hand On Tummy Exercise

a) Repeat the above exercise standing up without the book and only your hand against your tummy.

b) Breathe in to a 4 count filling up your tank and popping your tummy out towards your hand. Exhale to the count of 4 on *"huh,"* always being aware of the controlled exhalation with diaphragm manipulation in pulling your midsection back towards your backbone. This is the movement of the singer's breath standing up, or the position you will be singing from with your midsection purposely controlling the breathing in and out directions.

c) Repeat the exercise a couple of times with the 4 count breath in to fill up your tank and the 4 count breath out on the *"huh"* sound, always being aware of the controlled exhalation from your midsection towards your backbone.

d) Finally, complete the exercise by filling up your tank to the count of 4, and use your midsection to control the exhalation to the counts of 6, 8 and 10 respectively. Remember, the breath in will alway be to the count of 4: it will be the exhalation that varies in length just like different phrases in a song.

Duplicating the proper movement of *"air in/tummy out"* to note floating out on *"exhalation to flat tummy"* will take some thought, as you no longer have gravity helping you. When lying on your back, the book *"fell"* easily during the exhalation with a little help from gravity, but your diaphragm, or midsection resistance against the book, is ultimately what gave you the power to control how quickly the book fell with the exhalation. What you are achieving by the controlled movement and conscious manipulation of your midsection to move out and in while in a standing position is also known as *"Diaphragm Support,"* which we will discuss in **POINT 2.**

Open Throat Breathing Exercise

It is very important to keep the throat as open as possible when singing, creating an open pathway from your mid-section, or diaphragm, up to your mouth. To get the feeling of an open throat, emulate a yawn and try to stop from yawning at the last second. Hold this position and take deep slow breaths in and out through your mouth. This is the open feeling in the throat region that you want to experience when you sing. Using this technique will help you to avoid becoming a *"Squeezer"* as defined in the *"Troubleshooting"* section.

Puppy Pant Exercise

Now that you have the slow controlled movement of your midsection mastered, let's try quicker, shorter bursts of breathing. First, place your hand on your tummy. Next, fill your tank with air by taking in a singer's breath, then quickly pull in your abdominal area forcing the air to come out through your mouth on the *"huh"* sound. Let your tummy naturally pop back out to do many *"huhs"* in a row.

(This movement is similar to the Heimlich Maneuver which is used when someone is choking, but you will be doing it by yourself).

It will be a natural reaction for your tummy to pop back out instantly and for you to suck air back in through your mouth once you have forced all the air out of your *"tank,"* thus sounding like a *"puppy pant."* This is the first feeling of power you can achieve by simply using your breath. As we get deeper into how breathing and diaphragm support work together in **POINT 2**, you will understand this connection more.

STOP ANY BREATHING EXERCISE IF YOU FEEL DIZZY OR LIGHTHEADED!!!
Pace yourself as you are building stamina.

Refer to video tutorials:
"Warm Up Exercise #1" *(1-2-3-4-5-4-3-2-1 Exercise)*
"Warm Up Exercise #5" *(EE-EH-OH-OO-AH Exercise)*

Troubleshooting

What if you think you are taking in a singer's breath correctly, but things still aren't feeling effortless or "floaty"? The following diagnoses are potential challenges that you might be creating which are inhibiting correct breathing and movement of the singer's breath.

Be Aware Of Over Breathing

Although the "5 Point Singing System" teaches that breathing is the first and foremost point in successful singing, it is imperative that you do not "over breathe" in the delivery of a song. Learning to identify shorter phrases between breathmarks (which would require smaller breaths in) and longer phrases (which would require larger breaths in) will be very helpful in the precise and effortless delivery of a song.
(Am I starting to sound like a broken record yet? For you youngsters, it's kind of like hearing a musical loop…over and over and over…you get the picture). It is equally important to let go of any residual air from the previous breath before taking in a new breath. If you find yourself adding new air on top of leftover air from the previous breath, something I call "stacking" will occur, which is one way we sabotage our breathing. Stacking and other breathing challenges are identified in this "Troubleshooting" section.

Heads Up For "Backwards Breathing"

Backwards breathing occurs when the tummy does not fill up like a balloon when you take in a breath.
Instead, the tummy sucks in and goes flat while the shoulders go up as the breath comes in.
Also, the amount of air you can take in is minimal, which would only work for short phrases. Backwards breathing makes it impossible to sustain power or pitch correctly as it inhibits the amount of air you take in,
and air is the secret tool to successful effortless singing. You will understand this better once you have read **POINT 2 – DIAPHRAGM SUPPORT.** The bottom line is to be aware of the movement of your singer's breath. Always remember – "air in/tummy out" and you will avoid all sorts of problems.

Beware Singer Stumbling Block – "H Seepage"

A very common bad habit that occurs with beginner and seasoned singers alike is the "h seepage" of air before a vowel sound. This is a self-sabotaging habit that you will want to become aware of. When we absent-mindedly put an "h" sound before a word that starts with a vowel sound or before a vowel sound in the middle of a word, it depletes our air supply very quickly, thus leaving us with a shortage of air to support our pitch or diaphragm engagement [POINT 2]. Be very aware of this habit and try to hit the vowel purely, without adding an "h" sound before it. For example, sing "I love you" with an "h" in front of the "I" and pay attention to what it feels like: "hI love you." How much air escaped with that one simple and seemingly innocent action? Then repeat the phrase with no "h" in front of the "I". Did you have a lot more air left at the end of the phrase?

"The Stacker"

Stacking occurs when the singer forgets to let go of residual air from the previous breath and adds new air on top of left-over air. This will result in a sort of tightening of the neck and shoulders and create a "short of breath" feeling. Always make room for the new breath by depleting all your air in the previous phrase or consciously releasing any leftover air before taking in a new breath. You don't want to be a "Stacker."

"The Squeezer"

Keeping your airway open and unobstructed by not manipulating or squeezing the throat is very important for the notes to be able to "float out" on the breath. As a singer, you want the performance of a song to feel and sound as effortless in its delivery as possible. How many times have we heard a singer perform who makes our throat hurt by their straining? There are many reasons for straining which we will address in the coming POINTS. Regarding breathing, straining may be caused by squeezing off the air at the throat by physically tightening the throat and not letting the notes "float out" on the breath through a relaxed open throat. It can also be the result of the tongue going up at the back and shutting off part of the throat *(think aerial ski-jump platform)*. You want your tongue to lie as flat as possible in your lower palate. To have effortless, "floaty" notes, be aware of keeping the throat open. When it isn't open, I like to call this kind of singer a "Squeezer."

"The Hourglass Breather"

In my years of teaching, I have been able to identify and label the different kinds of breathing challenges. This one is the love-child of "The Squeezer" and "The Stacker," but it is a bit harder to identify. An "Hourglass Breather" is one who initially takes in a proper singer's breath, but then contracts their diaphragm. This constricts the air right in the middle of the tank, forming an hourglass shape, and ultimately restricts the singer to using only half the breath. The sensation is one of tightness or squeezing. When the "Hourglass Breather" takes in a new breath, they are only replacing the top half of the hourglass with air, which puts new air on top of old air creating the stacking issue. It is imperative that you breathe in, exhale all your air with the notes floating on it, then take in a new breath with no leftover air still hiding in your tank.

"The Faker"

Another type of breathing challenge that occurs often but a singer can be unaware of is faking a breath. This means the singer goes through the motions of leaving a space for taking in a breath but does not actually physically take in any air. After everything you have learned up to this point, you are probably figuring out that no air in means no power, lousy pitch due to lack of air support, and an overall sense of frustration over why things aren't working well. It all comes down to the cycle of air in/tummy out, notes that float out on the breath, a release of residual air, and finally inhalation of a new breath. This process is what I call "Air Exchange."

Air Exchange

Now that we have learned to do a singer's breath properly, we must realize how the exhalation of the breath helps our notes "float out" on the breath.

Refer to video tutorial **"Troubleshooting Your Breathing"**

POINT - 2
DIAPHRAGM SUPPORT

POINT 2 - DIAPHRAGM SUPPORT

Have you ever wondered what is going on when you are hiccupping? Hiccupping happens when the large muscle, called the diaphragm, goes into spasm. The diaphragm is a muscular band located mid-torso separating the chest and abdominal cavities. Learning to manipulate the movement of the diaphragm is the second secret to having great power and proper pitch support. In order to sing effectively and effortlessly, diaphragm support works hand and hand with the *"singer's breath,"* and one cannot be successful without the other.

Think of it this way: if we have no *"air in our tank"* when singing, the diaphragm will be unable to function properly in relation to support, pitch and power as it will have no fuel to use when it moves. When you get into the habit of breathing often and always having air in your tank, your diaphragm will be able to deliver the kind of support needed in a song at any particular moment. There is an exception to this rule, however, and it applies to the singing of your lowest notes.

Low-Range Notes

Every note in your range requires a different degree and variation of diaphragm support. The general rule of thumb is that diaphragm support becomes greater as you ascend in your vocal range. The speed at which you manipulate your diaphragm by pulling it in varies with different notes in your range as well. This manipulated movement also works hand in hand with where the note is resonating in your body. For example, in your low-range where the notes resonate in your chest, often called *"chest voice"* or *"chest placement,"* there is little to no diaphragm support used. The *air-to-tone ratio* of your voice is important in this range, too. You want to get into the idea of "speaking" your lowest notes rather than *"singing"* them. This is achieved by giving no or very little diaphragm support, meaning the diaphragm is completely relaxed and not engaged in any way. Also, you may not want to let too much diaphragm-supported air escape through your throat to *"pad"* the tone of your note in your super low and low ranges.

When you add diaphragm support in these ranges, you often end up forcing too much air out which may shoot the note sharp or make the note less audible than if you take the *"speak your low notes"* approach. There are exceptions to every general rule and the style and range of the song will often give you clues as to how the notes in certain ranges should be sung.

Occasionally, the *"no diaphragm support"* or *"no air around the tone"* theory isn't the approach that is best for the song. However, in most cases, it is the most effective way to deliver super low and low notes so that they *"read"* or register best on the microphone. The exception will come into play if a whispier tone is desired for emotional effect. It is then that you would deliver the note with a bit more air around the tone changing the air to tone ratio.

Mid-Range and Upper-Mid-Range Notes

In your mid to upper-mid range, the diaphragm support starts to *"kick in."* This typically starts in what I like to call the Full voice/Speaking tonality Resonance. When performing vocal exercises or singing a song, you will become aware of when to start engaging the diaphragm the moment you start to feel the notes become a bit strained. Having sufficient air in your tank will allow you to pull your diaphragm in towards your backbone on the challenging notes, helping you maintain correct placement so they can *"float"* out on the breath with good power and pitch. The higher you ascend in your range the faster and greater your diaphragm will pull in. If the whole line or *"phrase"* of the song is in your upper mid-range, a correctly engaged diaphragm will stay engaged, creating a sort of, *"platform"* for the other notes to sit on. If you let your diaphragm completely relax after pulling it in to support the first note, you will often sing flat the rest of the line. When you are at the top of your Chest/Full voice/Speaking voice range in what I call the *"Diva"* or *"Rockstar"* placement or *"zone,"* your diaphragm will be slammin' hard and fast towards your backbone to give you the power to stay in the right placement: something we will learn about in POINT 3 - PLACEMENT/RESONANCE. This major diaphragm movement is like a self-propelled *Heimlich Maneuver,* which I sometimes also refer to as *"calling voice."* To better understand this powerful type of diaphragm support, pretend you are calling *(not yelling – big difference)* the word *"hey"* to someone across a busy street. What is physically happening to your body? If you are an effective *"caller,"*

what you are doing is:

    a) taking in a great big Singer's Breath which is filling up your tank,

    b) pulling your diaphragm in towards your backbone very quickly and with purpose, then

    c) expelling the air with the force of this movement projecting your voice in a powerful way as the notes float out on the breath through an open relaxed throat.

When using calling voice, be aware of keeping your throat open, letting the air pass easily through your throat and not squeezing in any way. This is essentially the way "Divas" and "Rockstars" hit those big notes: it takes a lot of effort. These songs are like a marathon of breathing and diaphragm support, in that you will breathe frequently, use up a large capacity of your air tank per phrase, and experience significant diaphragm movement. If you are a lazy person, I suggest you sing only lullabies to babies as you won't be effective as a Diva or Rockstar unless you put the effort in to get that diaphragm support rockin'!

High-Range Notes

There is an area of placement/resonance which we will learn about in POINT 3 called "the Mask Area." This placement is often used in classical performance and features a gentler, higher, lighter and airier tone than the Diva or Rockstar placement. The diaphragm support needed here changes to a slower, more controlled movement without any sudden pulls toward the backbone. A "platform" is created by almost pushing downward with your diaphragm like a plunger. This "pushing down on the plunger" feeling creates a more fluid, elongated kind of air support than the more abrupt pulls required in the Diva/Rockstar placement. The notes in this higher range should float out with a more effortless, lighter sensation. Think of a column of air that supports a ping-pong ball floating on top of it: it is smooth and controlled, not fast and "jerky."

It is very important to keep noting that the song will tell you what it requires from you to perform it with correct diaphragm support. If you tend to be more of a "lazy diaphragm" singer and do not engage the proper diaphragm support for upper mid-range notes, your body will automatically default to a different placement than what should be used, which may not be right for the song. For example, if you are singing a kickin' rock song and don't engage enough diaphragm support in the form of your calling voice to powerfully sustain your upper mid-range notes, your brain will automatically flip you into the lighter "Mask Area" placement when you should be staying in Diva/Rockstar. The difference in sound will be akin to a person singing a gentle folk song in front of 20,000 people at a rock concert. Okay, this example is extreme, but you get the picture. The "folk singer" is the wrong choice for the rock concert, where a rockstar performance is expected. You will understand this analogy better in POINT 3.

High-Range/Powerful Notes

Finally, there is one more placement which I have deemed "Supermask" that requires yet another variation of diaphragm support. This powerful high range delivery is a combination of Mask Area placement (POINT 3) and Diva/Rockstar diaphragm support *(faster and more intense).* Essentially, this combination creates a softer-edged version of the Diva/Rockstar placement and tone. What happens with this combination is that you add some major power to the lighter, airier mask tonality to create a less edgy sounding tone to the voice, but still generate some power out of this higher range. I first started hearing this placement with artists like **Leona Lewis** in her song, "Bleeding Love." Listen to the chorus where she flips into her mask area on *"keep bleedin', keep, keep bleedin.'"* She then flips back to her chest/full voice placement on the words "I" and "love" without losing any power, which typically happens with traditional mask placement.

This approach also adds an emotional urgency to the delivery of the song without feeling out of place. In this particular song, if she had stayed in powerful Diva placement she would likely have produced an overly edgy sound. Once again, I always say the style or production of the song will tell you what is required of you technically and emotionally to deliver it perfectly. You will understand more about placements and how they work with diaphragm support in our next chapter, **POINT 3** - PLACEMENT/RESONANCE.

The diaphragm support that is required to perform a song correctly becomes clearer when we map it out on the same lyric sheet where we mapped out our breath marks. I like to use a sideways "v" under the words or syllables that require me to engage my diaphragm. The more support I need on a word, the darker or bigger I make the "v". Again, you are mapping out your lyrics so that you know exactly where and when you need to breathe and support with your diaphragm when navigating your way through a song. This is an incredibly effective tool in learning how to perform a new song.

Refer to video tutorials:
"Diaphragm Support"
"Warm Up Exercise #6" *(BEE BEE BEE BEE Exercise)*

Mapping Out Your Diaphragm Support

Figure 2 below is the chorus of **Ain't No Mountain High Enough** with breathmarks from POINT 1 and diaphragm support symbols.

Figure 2

(√ = breath and < = diaphragm "pull")

√'Cause Baby there

    <

√Ain't no mountain high enough

<   <

√Ain't no valley low enough

<   <

√Ain't no river wide enough

<   <

√To keep me from gettin' to you Babe

   <

As you can see in the map above, the "√" is used to indicate a breath at the beginning of each phrase and the "<" symbol in various sizes situated underneath specific words or syllables represents how big the diaphragm pull should be at that moment. Following this "mapped out" lyric sheet is a sure fire way to sing the song with great pitch and emotion.

Refer to video tutorial **"Mapping Out Your Lyrics"**

DIAPHRAGM EXERCISES:

Diaphragm Exercise 1 - Motor Boat Lips

To see if you are connected to your diaphragm, take in a big breath as if sucking in air through a tube, remembering the direction of the singer's breath from POINT 1. Once you have a full tank of air, try to pull your diaphragm muscle back gently towards your backbone passing air through relaxed, closed, lips making them vibrate to create a "motor boat" sound. If you have trouble at first, try using short bursts of air by pulsing your diaphragm quickly towards your backbone. This movement is similar to the puppy pant described in the breathing exercises, but with a different mouth position. If you can make the motor boat sound, you are connecting with your diaphragm support: just be sure to stop if you feel dizzy. If you can't make the sound initially, don't get frustrated: it will come in time.

Diaphragm Exercise 2 – "1-2-3-4-5-4-3-2-1-5-1" Exercise

On the first five notes of a major scale (think "do, re, me, fah, so"), sing the numbers forward from 1 to 5 then backwards to 1, adding a 5-1 jump at the end to get an idea of how much you need to engage your diaphragm to render the final 5 note pitch-perfect. The higher you ascend in your range, the more you will engage your diaphragm to make the correct pitch of each note. Change to the vowel sound "ee" when a note starts feeling a little strained and where you have to start engaging more diaphragm movement.

Refer to video tutorial "Warm Up Exercise #3" (1-2-3-4-5-4-3-2-1-5-1 Exercise)

Diaphragm Exercise 3 – "Huh Huh" Exercise

On the same note, sing five little pulses of the sound "huh," pulling in your diaphragm as much as you can on the final one while singing it increasingly louder. This isn't the prettiest sounding exercise – in fact, I call it "the dying duck in the thunder storm" exercise for that reason. That said, it will give you an idea of how manipulating your diaphragm can help with pitch accuracy and potential power. Repeat this exercise while ascending higher in your range. Change to the vowel sound "hee" as you ascend to create a more forward placement in your vocal path (Point 4) alleviating any strain you may be starting to feel.

Diaphragm Exercise 4 - The 1-5 Exercise On "Huh"

In this exercise we make the 1-5 jump of a major scale on the word "huh." We do it in two patterns with a small breath in between. To try this, sing "huh" (1) "huh" (5) "huh" (1) "huh" (5) "huh" (1) "huh" (5) "huh" (1) *(take in a small breath here)* then repeat the pattern. Your diaphragm support will become very noticeable each time you sing the 5, as the pulls toward your backbone will become much more pronounced.

Refer to video tutorial **"Warm Up Exercise #2"** *(1-5 Exercise)*

Repeat this exercise ascending higher in your range with each of the 1-5 combinations. Once you are unable to go any higher in your Diva/Rockstar placement and need to flip up into your Mask Area, the pulls will be gentler and not so defined but more like the plunger feeling diaphragm support I outlined earlier in this chapter. Also, in this range, you will want to change the vowel sound to "hee" to make it easier to sing.
Because of the 5 note span, you will have areas of the exercise where the 1 will be in your Diva/Rockstar Placement with the substantial diaphragm support and the 5 of the exercise will be in the Mask Area Placement with the plunger like support.

Air To Tone Ratio

In summary, diaphragm support is used to achieve pitch accuracy, proper placement of the voice, projection and power. There is one more thing diaphragm support can manipulate, however, and that is the tone of the voice. Regulating the amount of air that escapes around the tone by engaging different levels of diaphragm support is something I call "air-to-tone ratio." Learning to control the air-to-tone ratio of your voice is particularly important when singing with others in order to create a blend of voices, or for infusing certain notes with emotional value.

Earlier in POINT 2 we discussed creating a wispier tone by letting more air escape with the tone of the voice. This is achieved by consciously engaging a larger diaphragm pull towards the backbone, forcing more air out around the tone. To visualize this process, think of your diaphragm support like bellows used to stoke a fire. If you want a slight air flow, the movement needs to be smaller; if you want more air, the movement needs to be much more substantial. Remember, for a wispier tone using diaphragm support, the initial uptake of air at the appropriate breathmark will have to be significant. To achieve power and projection from the diaphragm support minus the wispiness, still draw in a substantial breath, but simply adjust the air-to-tone ratio by preventing the larger amount of air from escaping around the tone. Experiment with singing a note with pure tone, a **50%** mix of air and tone, and finally a pure air only sounding note with very little tone engaged.

REMEMBER TO STOP IF YOU FEEL DIZZY OR LIGHTHEADED – YOU ARE BUILDING UP STAMINA!

POINT - 3
PLACEMENT / RESONANCE

POINT 3 - PLACEMENT/RESONANCE

As we have touched upon in **POINT 2 - Diaphragm Support,** there are five predominant placements, or resonating zones, of the voice. Remember that each placement requires a specific diaphragm support for it to be most effective. To achieve correct diaphragm support, the right amount of air per singer's breath needs to be taken in for each individual phrase, as was outlined in **POINT 1 - Breathing.** Are you starting to see how these points are dependent on each other to help a singer deliver a song perfectly? To help establish the connection, let's revisit the placements we first discussed in **POINT 2.**

Chest Placement

In our low and low-mid-range notes, the vocal cords are thick and vibrate slowly as the voice resonates in our chest cavity.
To experience this, sing a low *"AH"* and put your hand on your chest feeling the vibration. Just a reminder, in this part of your range the diaphragm support is minimal but will start to kick in when you ascend into the mid-range *"Full Voice/Speaking Tonality"* placement of your voice.

Full Voice/Speaking Tonality Placement

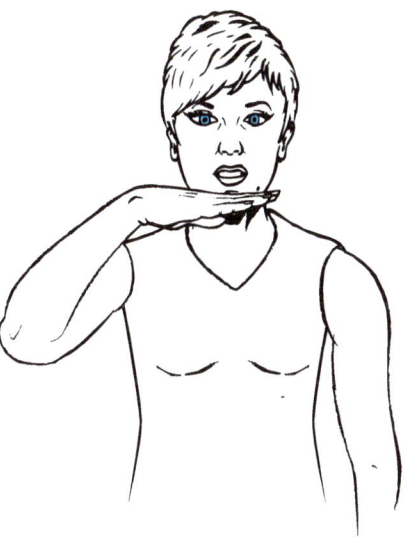

Once we ascend into our mid-range notes, the placement of the voice should move towards our oral cavity, avoiding a rest stop in the throat area. The mid-range notes are what I usually refer to as *"Full Voice"* or *"Speaking Tonality"* placement or resonance, and sit just below the Diva/Rockstar notes in the vocal range. Avoid placing this range in your throat as doing so can create all sorts of vocal challenges and problems *(I like to call this type of throat singer a "Tucker," something we will discuss in POINT 4 - Vocal Path).* When moving from lower-range to mid-range, you want to focus on making a *"jump"* from the chest placement over your throat and into the lower oral cavity. This is achieved by activating diaphragm support, which will, in effect, catapult your voice to the correct placement.

Diva/Rockstar Placement

At the top end of our Full Voice/Speaking Tonality placement is an area I have named the "Diva/Rockstar" placement. If you were to think of your vocal range as a thermometer, this would start in the upper middle of it.

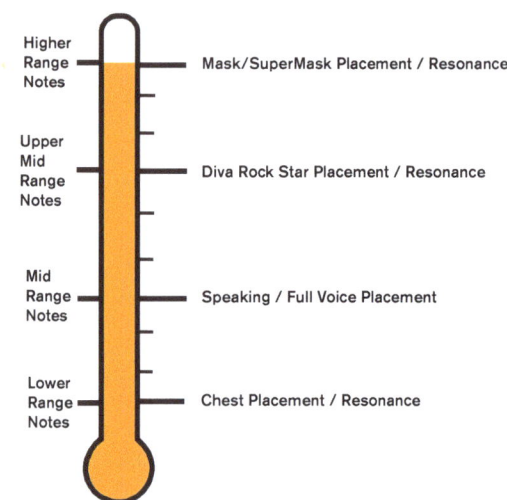

When in this placement, your voice resonates in the top of your oral cavity both below and in front of your nose, depending on what vowel sound you are singing. Again, avoid trying to place this range in your throat. Precise placement is achieved by activating the correct diaphragm support. This placement can best be demonstrated by pretending to call to a person across a busy street. Remember the "calling voice" analogy in **POINT 2?** This kind of support requires frequent breathing and breath capacity awareness coupled with quick, strong diaphragm pulls toward your backbone to project your voice. Remember, however, that this placement is like "calling," not "yelling."

The Diva/Rockstar tone is one of power as it is the top end of your full voice. It relies on shorter, thinner, more quickly-vibrating vocal chords and resonates right around what we all feel as the "break" in our voice *(which can sometimes sound like a 13-year-old boy going through a voice change).* The easiest way to deal with our break area is to flip up into our Mask Area placement without engaging the major diaphragm support required to stay in Diva/Rockstar placement. However, jammin' out on *(as in not engaging)* the diaphragm power and defaulting to Mask Area placement doesn't always fit the style of the song we are singing.

Our goal is to be able to sing those break notes either in full Diva/Rockstar voice with power using the big diaphragm support or in Mask Area with a lighter tonality using the "plunger"- like, more gentle diaphragm support. In terms of knowing which placement to use, the song you have chosen to perform will dictate. For example, you can't sing Aretha Franklin's song, "R-E-S-P-E-C-T" in mask area or you will sound like an opera singer trying to sing Rhythm and Blues. Conversely, you wouldn't sing a **Sarah McLachlan** song with the maxed out diaphragm support required to stay in Diva placement.

Mask Area Placement

When we get that feeling that we can't sing any higher in our full voice, we automatically flip up into our "Mask Area" placement. The diaphragm support required in this zone is much gentler than that of Diva/Rockstar. Once you take in a breath, you engage the diaphragm to plunge downwards as we touched on in POINT 2, creating a platform of air for the Mask Area notes to sit on. This movement is therefore far less dramatic than what is required for Diva/Rockstar diaphragm support. Interestingly, there are many singers such as **Sarah McLachlan** and **Dido** who flip from Full Voice placement into Mask Area placement for a note or line to add emotional nuances to their song delivery.

To find your Mask Area placement/resonance, put two fingers on either side of your nose and do a "puppy whine" or hum starting from high in your range descending to your mid-range. There will be notes in this higher range where you will feel a vibration or buzz in your face and fingers -- this is your Mask Area. In this upper-range of the voice, your vocal cords are very thin, very short and vibrating very quickly. For a visual reference, think about what a full balloon does when you stretch the neck and start to let the air seep out slowly, creating a high-pitched sound where the top of the balloon is tight and vibrating quickly. At the other end of the spectrum, if you let a balloon go, the neck is loose and you get a lower sound (perhaps like someone who ate beans for lunch? LOL) while the air flows out because the neck is vibrating more slowly. This is very similar to what is going on with your vocal cords in the ranges described above.

Supermask Placement

"Supermask" feels exactly like Mask Area placement, but just with different diaphragm support. In other words, Supermask is a hybrid of the Mask Area placement and Diva/Rockstar diaphragm support.

By engaging the more aggressive diaphragm support of Diva/Rockstar, we are able to get a bigger sound out of the Mask Area placement without the edgier more aggressive Diva/Rockstar tone. The marriage of Mask Area placement and Diva/Rockstar diaphragm support to create the Supermask sound adds yet another vocal nuance we can use if a song requires it. Try not to use Supermask, however, as a lazy way of singing your top notes in true Diva/Rockstar songs that should sound bigger or more edgy.

(You don't want to sound like the church lady trying to sing rock and roll.)

Refer to video tutorials:

"Placement/Resonance"

"Correct Placement For The Song"

POINT 4 – VOCAL PATH

The vocal path is the direction that your voice takes once you initiate a note by taking in a singer's breath, engage the diaphragm support in varying degrees, and pass air through the vocal cords to create tone. In my world, there are three predominant vowel sound columns or *"vocal paths"*: "AH" "EE" and "OO." Understanding the various vocal paths and how to direct them is important when diagnosing vocal challenges and formulating proper vocal technique.

The "AH" Vocal Path

When we take in a singer's breath and sing the "AH" vowel sound, the vocal path created is one that goes straight up to mid head where the sound of the note seems to reside, just above the top of the head as noted in *Figure 5.* The vocal path should naturally move more forward as we ascend in our vocal range to make it easier to sing, regardless of what word or vowel sound we actually are singing. However, some singers resist the urge to let the vocal path move as they ascend in their vocal range, creating some major stumbling blocks.

Figure 1: The "AH" Mouth Shape

The "EE" Vocal Path

The second vocal path, created with the "EE" vowel sound, is achieved by directing the sound column in a more forward direction, towards the eye and forehead area *(Figure 5).* As a singer, you want to gravitate towards this vocal path when you begin to feel any strain or stress in your mid-range notes and higher. When we take in a singer's breath, engage diaphragm support, then sing the vowel sound "EE," we can hear the vibration out in front of the eye/forehead area rather than in the "mid head" where the "AH" vocal path is located.

Vocal Path Exercise 1

To get an idea of how the "AH" and "EE" vocal paths differ, choose a note in your upper-mid range and sing "AH" to "EE" back and forth 3 or 4 times. You should be able to feel the vocal path rolling forward along your hard palate, also known as the roof of your mouth. Experiment with this exercise in different ranges of your voice to see if you can feel the vocal paths more distinctly from one range to the other. It is also really important that you form the vowel shapes properly. When singing the "AH" vowel sound, think of the "AH" sound in the word "saw" with your jaw dropped making an oval shape of your mouth. Or, think of when the doctor sticks a tongue depressor in your mouth and says, "say AH" *(Figure 1).* If you are leaning more to the "A" sound, as in the word "apple," the sides of your mouth will be pulling back. You want to avoid this as it creates a tight feeling that makes it more difficult to sing effortlessly. Look at yourself in the mirror until you can make the correct shapes naturally.

Figure 2:
The "EE" Mouth Shape

Refer to video tutorial **"Warm Up Exercise #7"** *(AH-EE Exercise)*

It is equally important when singing the "EE" vowel sound to keep the sides of your mouth relaxed and your jaw dropped. Doing so will allow you to modify the "EE" vowel sound, making it easier to sing as you ascend in your range *(Figure 2).* Again, with this vowel sound, be aware of not pulling the sides of your mouth back towards your ears and baring your teeth like a cheeky chimpanzee, as doing so will make effortless singing a challenge *See Figure 3.* I have always scratched my head at vocal coaches who encourage their students to "smile" broadly when they are singing. This creates major tightness and strain in the mouth and throat area and leads to frustration when trying to sing a note, especially an "EE" vowel sound in a higher range.

Figure 3:
"Chimpanzee" Mouth Shape
WRONG!

The "OO" Vocal Path

The "OO" vowel sound *(in words like "food", "shoe" and "true")* resonates more around the mouth area *(Figure 5)*.

To experience this feeling, sing an "OO" and pay attention to where you hear the sound residing. The "OO" vocal path seems to sit below the "EE" vocal path of the eye and forehead area and is already far forward without being too nasal-sounding. The feeling of the "OO" vocal path seems to stay under the nose regardless of what range you are singing in. It is also hard to tuck the "OO" sound back towards the "AH" vocal path.

"OO" is the vocal path that, in my opinion, is the most effortless path to find and doesn't seem to cause many challenges for the singer. When singing the actual "OO" sound, just be aware of not closing your mouth too tightly; instead, keep the cheeks relaxed in order to let the vowel sound "float" *(Figure 4)*.

Once again, remember that in order to get the desired results, your breathing and diaphragm support have to be working correctly as well.

Figure 4:
The "OO" Mouth Shape

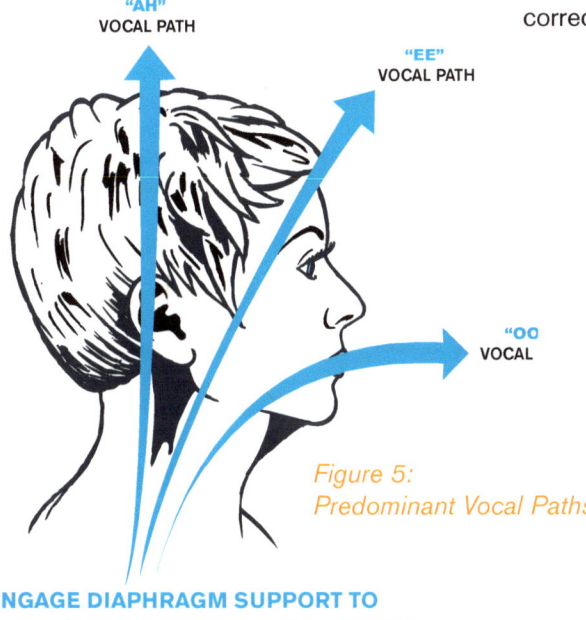

Figure 5:
Predominant Vocal Paths

ENGAGE DIAPHRAGM SUPPORT TO RELEASE SINGER'S BREATH HELPING THE NOTE TO FOLLOW VOCAL PATH

Vocal Path Exercise 2

As in Vocal Path Exercise 1 where we explored how the "AH" and "EE" vocal paths differ, choose a note in your upper-mid range and this time, slowly sing "AH" to "EE" to "OO." Roll back towards the "EE" and "AH" vocal paths all on one breath, and repeat this progression 3 or 4 times. Remember to take in the right amount of air and engage the right amount of diaphragm support *(are you tired of hearing this yet?).*
You should be able to feel the vocal path rolling forward along your hard palate from the "AH" to the "EE," and downward towards your mouth when you sing the "OO." You should then feel it roll up and back when you reverse the order of the vowel sounds. Experiment with different vocal ranges for this exercise to see if the feeling is more predominant in one more than another.

Remember, when directing these vocal paths, it is really important to pay attention to the formation of the vowel sounds. Keep your jaw dropped on the "AH" vowel sound to create an oval shaped mouth.
Also, be aware of not pulling the sides of your mouth back towards your ears when singing the "EE" vowel. The "OO" vowel sound mouth shape is one of a smaller circle, but not too tight.

Refer to video tutorial "Vocal Path"

Working In The Degrees of The Vocal Path

Other than the three most predominant vocal paths mentioned above, there are "notches," or varying degrees of vocal path, in between each of these vowel sounds as well, enabling the singer to place the note somewhere between each vocal path/vowel sound. It will take a little experimentation to find the right vocal paths for your voice and range. Most people have natural approximate vocal paths and seldom have to think about the paths' directions. However, there comes a singer every so often who strains to reach the notes. A person who strains in their upper-mid range and higher notes may be tilting their vocal path too far back towards the "AH" vocal path residence. Because of this positioning, I call these people "Tuckers." You know you are listening to a "Tucker" when your throat start to feel tight listening to them try to hit their high notes in Full/Speaking or Diva/Rockstar placements.

When working with a "Tucker," I coach them to sing the whole song on the "EE" vowel sound. This approach brings their voice much more forward in their head towards their eye and forehead area, to the front of the hard palate. Sometimes I will get them there by telling them to aim for the back of their upper teeth, which also is an effective way to find the "EE" vocal path. What this does is open up an unobstructed path to great soaring heights with the voice – an "elevator to the top," so to speak. The reason this shifting of the vocal path works is because they have tilted it forward towards the "EE," not straight up through the head as with the "AH" path. So, when they take in a singer's breath, engage their diaphragm in Diva/Rockstar placement then hit their high notes, there is no "ceiling," like the hard palate, to stop them from going *higher and Higher and HIGHER!*

I love to see a student's eyes get bigger and bigger when I have had them tilt their vocal path forward so that they can proceed to sing higher and higher in their Diva/Rockstar range, hitting notes they never dreamed possible. Remember that breathing, diaphragm support, and placement *(all the POINTS we have discussed so far)* have to be aligned and working together to create this incredible feeling of effortless power. Once the student has discovered this feeling, however, by singing the entire song on the "EE" vowel sound in the "EE" vocal path a few times, I then have them sing the actual lyrics, re-capturing the "EE" vocal path that has them soaring to new heights.

In contrast to "Tuckers," there are singers who seem to sing right out of their noses and sound nasally. This type of singer is too far forward in their nasal cavity and has to tilt back towards the "AH" vocal path a bit to get out of their nose and back on the correct vocal path – somewhere between the "AH" and the "EE" paths. This is where the varying degrees or notches come in *(Figure 6)* It may be that the singer only needs to tilt back a notch or two to find the desired vocal path. Balance, however, remains key. If they tilt too far back to the "AH" path, especially when singing higher notes, they could actually become a "Tucker," shifting from one extreme to the other.

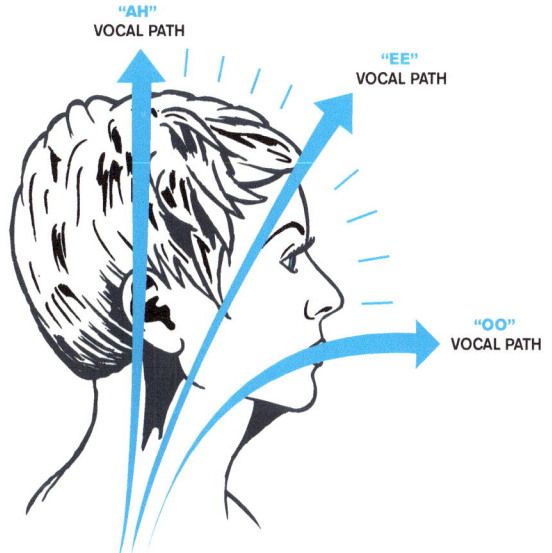

Figure 6: Varying Degrees of Vocal Path

Whenever I do exercises with my students, I always switch to the "EE" sound as we are ascending into the upper-mid range so we achieve the right vocal path for this area of the voice and alleviate any strain that may start to happen. If you find that you are straining on a word or line of your song, try singing the trouble spot on the vowel sound "EE," memorize how and where it "feels" in relation to the vocal paths and then sing the words with that same physical feeling. It is almost impossible to tuck an "EE" sound, so this is especially helpful for those of you who are "Tuckers" *(admitting it is the first step to fixing it!!!).*

Be aware of proper breathing, diaphragm support and staying in the appropriate placement *(not taking the easy way out by flipping up into Mask Area placement if you are meant to stay in Diva/Rockstar placement – think of the "calling voice" analogy)* to make it all come together.

Refer to video tutorial **"Warm Up Exercise #4"** *(AH-EE-AH-EE Exercise)*

POINT - 5
VOWEL MODIFICATION

POINT 5 – VOWEL MODIFICATION

Vowel modification is the act of manipulating the shape of your mouth to open up the vowel sound, allowing the note to float out more easily on the breath. If you are not aware of modifying your vowels, you will get the sense that the higher notes in a song will not be in your range due to the strain the unmodified vowels create. Magically, by modifying the vowels, the notes will be easier to sing and you will be able to deliver higher notes than you thought possible – especially in your Diva/Rockstar placement.

Modification can be achieved on almost any vowel sound by adding an *"h"* after the vowel and then dropping the jaw to relax the throat, thus creating space in the mouth to make the vowel *"taller"* or more open. Sometimes modification will change the actual vowel sound to another. For example, the word *"love"* is probably one of the most frequently sung words in popular music. The phonetic way to spell *"love"* is *"luv."*

The modified way to spell *"love"* is *"IAHv".* Sing the phonetic version and then sing the modified version. Which one felt more open and relaxed? Pay particular attention to the sound of the vowels. In the word *"love,"* the vowel is an *"o,"* but really, it sounds like an *"ah"* once you drop the jaw. The secret to vowel modification is that you *think* the modified vowel sound so your brain will make the mouth shape, and then you *sing* the word the way it is originally spelled. *Kooky, eh?* Trust me, it really works. I have had so many singers come through my door who don't know why they can't hit any Diva/Rockstar notes without straining. Once I hear that they have proper breathing, diaphragm support, placement, and no vocal path issues, *(POINTS 1-4),* I realize vowel modification is what's needed – such an easy fix when you know how to do it.

If you have watched the virtual vocal lesson DVD included with this manual, you probably noticed that I had you change to the *"EE"* vowel sound in your mid range to bring your vocal path forward, and then I started saying, *"Drop your jaw"* as you ascended in your range. *Why do you think I did that?* You got it – so you would modify the vowel and make it easier to sing in that range. Let's talk about different vowel sounds and how to best modify them.

The "A" Vowel Sounds

As with most vowels, there is a short sound, a long sound, and variations on these when vowels are combined. The word "apple" is an example of the "short A" sound. Say the word and pay attention to what your mouth is doing: the sides of your mouth pull back slightly, creating a subtle tightness. Next, say the word "saw" (which rhymes with "AH"), and note how the jaw drops and the sides of the mouth are more relaxed. We know by now that we want to alleviate any tightness in our mouth and throat area, so the "AH" sound becomes a way to achieve this. I once used this pairing of "short A" and "AH" to help my friend Leslie Alexander get over some performance angst. She's a great singer/songwriter who would get spooked by a line in her Diva placement in her song, "Garden In The Stones." When I listened to her, I realized that she had the first 4 POINTS right, but wasn't modifying the vowel on the word "plant" – instead, it sounded more like "plyant." Her mouth and throat were tight, and she became afraid of the line every time she had to sing it. Once I had her drop her jaw, think "plAHnt" but sing "plant," she never had trouble with it again - simple adjustment, major achievement.

Vowel Modification Exercise 1 – "Short A" to "AH"

a) On one note in your mid-range, sing the "short A" (as in "apple") vowel sound then switch to the vowel sound "AH" (as in "saw"). What you should be experiencing is a tight-side-of-mouth-pulled-back feeling when singing the "short A" sound, followed by a dropped-jaw, more relaxed feeling when singing the "AH" sound.

b) Memorize how the mouth shape of the "AH" sound feels, but sing "short A" when your mouth is in that "AH" shape. Feel a difference? Hear a difference in the pronunciation? What you should be experiencing is a more open/taller vowel position in your mouth shape and very little change in the pronunciation of the "short A." Remember, this is achieved by thinking the "AH" but singing the "short A."

c) Repeat this exercise, ascending higher into your Diva/Rockstar placement. It should be fairly easy to sing that "short A" sound higher and higher with little strain if you are thinking "AH."
Watch yourself in the mirror to be sure you are changing the shape of your mouth by dropping the jaw. For best results, don't forget to breathe and support with your diaphragm.

Another prominent "A" vowel sound is the "long A." In my world, that is modified to "EH," as in, "I'm Canadian, eh!". Again, by thinking "EH," you are dropping the jaw and relaxing the sides of your mouth, making the vowel sound easier to sing. Note that there is a slight "y" sound at the end of this "EH" pronunciation.

What this creates is two vowel sounds in one called a "dipthong." You want to avoid closing down on the second vowel sound "y" by bringing your jaw up. Keeping the jaw relaxed while singing the second vowel in the dipthong leaves the vowel open and "floaty." With this in mind, if I were mapping out some words on my lyric sheet to remind me to open up the vowels on the "long A" sound, I might write the following:

"Baby" = "Behbeh"   "take" = "tehk"   "place" = "plehs"

The "E" Vowel Sounds

Let's think about how many "E" vowel sounds there are. Words like "egg" and "elephant" have a "short E" sound: when you say or sing them, your jaw is already dropping so that the vowel already floats. The "long E" sound *(as in "see")* is quite the opposite, however, and needs to be modified in order for it to float out effortlessly. The exercise below will help train your brain in how to do this.

Vowel Modification Exercise 2 – "EE" to "EH"

a) On one note in your mid-range, sing the vowel sound "EE," then switch to the vowel sound "EH" *(again, as in "Canadian, eh!")*. What you should be experiencing is a tight-side-of-mouth-pulled-back feeling when singing the "EE" sound, followed by a dropped-jaw, more relaxed feeling when singing the "EH" sound.

b) Memorize the way the mouth shape feels with the "EH" sound, but sing "EE" when your mouth is in that "EH" shape. *Feel a difference? Hear a difference in the pronunciation?* What you should be experiencing is a more open/taller vowel position in your mouth shape and very little change in the pronunciation of "EE". Remember, this is achieved by thinking the "EH" but singing the "EE."

c) Repeat this exercise, ascending higher into your Diva/Rockstar placement. It should be fairly easy to sing that "EE" sound higher and higher with little strain if you are thinking "EH."
Watch yourself in the mirror to be sure you are changing the shape of your mouth by dropping the jaw. Again, don't forget to breathe and support with your diaphragm for best results.

The "I" Vowel Sounds

As was the case with the "short E" sound, the "short I" sound (as in "it," "win," and "lovin'") basically modifies itself as it is already in a dropped-jaw position. This is an instance where a subtle "h" naturally comes in after the vowel (as in "iHt," "wiHn," "lAHviHn"). If you do find yourself having difficulty with the "short I" sound, experiment with leaning a bit more towards an "AH" mouth shape to alleviate any strain.

With the "long I" sound, adjusting for a "dipthong" that we've already mentioned, becomes important. To elaborate, a dipthong is the term we use to describe one vowel sound that merges subtly or more obviously into two when sung or spoken. Some examples of "long I" sound dipthongs include "wide," "try," and "mine," in that with each word, the "long I" merges into an "EE" or "Y" sound when pronounced. While the "long A" hinted at being a dipthong with its slight "y" at the end of the vowel, the "long I" is a definite example of a pure dipthong with its "I-EE." This double vowel sound is one of the most challenging to sing but easiest to modify following the procedure described below.

Vowel Exercise 3 – "I-EE" to "AH-y"

This one is going to pop up a lot in your vocalizing. How many times do you think you will sing the word "I" in the course of a lifetime? A lot. You will find this word especially tight in the Diva/Rockstar placement, so it is imperative that you modify it to sing it effortlessly.

a) On one note in your upper mid-range, sing the vowel sound "I-EE." What you should be experiencing is a tight-side-of-mouth-pulled-back feeling and a bit of a strain to hit such a note.

b) You should now be familiar with the "AH" vowel mouth shape if you have done the preceding exercises. The way to modify the "I-EE" is to sing the "AH" and then close the vowel sound at the very last moment with a slight "y" sound. Try it. What you should be experiencing is a more open/taller vowel position in your mouth shape and a slight change in the pronunciation. Instead of going to the "EE" sound almost immediately after engaging the "I," you let the "AH" ring and close it at the very end with the smaller, less dominant "y" sound. You will still convey the "I," but it will float so much more easily.

This modification should be used on any word in any range that has this particular dipthong sound *(e.g., "I," "right," "mine," "midnight").* If I were mapping out these words on my lyric sheet, I would note the following modifications:

"I" = "AHy"   *"right" – "rAHyt"*   *"mine" – "mAHyn"*   *"midnight" –"mihdnAHyt"*

The "O" Vowel Sound

By now you may be getting the sense that many of the vowel sounds are interchangeable, regardless of the modification. The "short O" is no exception. Say the word "octopus" – what first vowel sound do you notice? You got it – the "AH." Similarly, the "long O" *(as in "over," "only," and "grow")* is partially modified already, in that it is not as tight as the "EE" sound but half way open to the modified sound.

What you need to remember with the "long O" vowel sound is that the higher you ascend in your range, the more your jaw should drop to create the full open/tall vowel sensation.

This will actually feel a little like you are singing somewhere between "OHw" and "AHw." So, if you are straining with this vowel, think "AHw" but sing the "long O," keeping your mouth relaxed and fairly open.

Here is what mapped-out, modified "long O" words might look like:

"over" = "AHwvahr"   *"only" = "AHwnleh"*   *"grow" = "grAHw"*

The "U" Vowel Sound

Are you sensing a pattern here with the "short" vowel sounds? Say the word "umbrella." Oh, big surprise: the "short U" can be modified with the "AH" sound again – "AHm-brAH-lAH." The "AH" in fact opens up all the vowel sounds in the word whether it is the "short U," "short E," or "short A." Now for the "long U" vowel sound - this one is a bit tricky, as it tends to be somewhat tight. When I sing a pure "long U" sound before modification, I feel tension from the middle of my neck up to my jaw. A quick and simple way to alleviate this strain is – you guessed it – to drop your jaw. With the "long U," you will want to think "yOH" but sing "you," bringing the sides of your mouth in slightly at the end of the vowel sound. Try it: it really makes a world of difference in the effortless delivery of the vowel. Some modifications might be written out like this:

"true" = "trOH"   *"tune" = "tOHn"*   *"united" = "yOHnAHytAHd*

Summary

In summary, we have learned to modify some of the basic vowel sounds. While there are many other vowel combinations that could be accounted for, doing so would require a manual of its own. I'll therefore conclude this section with the following advice: use your ears, drop and relax your jaw and experiment with the vowel sounds to find the modification that works best with the words you are singing. In addition, always remember the vowel modification mantra: think the adjustment, but sing the actual vowel – a method that works for all combinations.

Enough About Vowels - What About Consonants?

A funny thing about consonants – you need to add them to the vowels to form words *(unless you live in Poland)*. In my world, consonants are used to "close" the vowel sound. When you do finally get to a consonant, be aware of how soon you close the vowel sound and how long you dwell on that consonant. I am a firm believer that hanging onto the vowels a little longer, making them open and tall, then closing quickly with the consonant is the best way to get notes to float. I always think of the vowel being football-shaped, and when you get to the narrow point at the end of the ball, that is the consonant. Of course, there are always exceptions to this way of thinking, especially when trying to sing with stylistic nuances – something considered in the next section.

Consonants and Music Style

Over the last few years I have paid particular attention to the differentiating nuances of musical styles, and I've found that the treatment of consonants, especially as they relate to vowels, is quite significant. To better understand this idea, let's talk about country music for a minute. There are many country artists who come from a part of the world where people speak, and therefore sing, with an accent we often hear referred to as a "drawl." Perhaps it is because of this drawl that consonants in the words of country songs often seem more pronounced.

For example, a word like "girl" might sound more like "gerl," a pronunciation that shortens the vowel sound and lands hard and lingers on the "r." Let's now take the same word and vowel/consonant relationship to a different style. In a soulful R&B ballad, the word "girl" might sound more like "gahl," sung with hardly any "r" enunciation, thus creating softer edges around the word. The vowel sound would be modified to be open, "floaty," and sustained for as long as possible, while the consonant would be clipped and short, closing off the vowel at the very last moment. This is typical R&B styling, and another example of how vowels and consonants can be married for stylizing purposes.

While the examples just mentioned explore the ways speech patterns and accents may influence vocal styles, please note that if you don't speak with a particular type of accent, don't assume one when singing. I am all about *"singing it like you speak it,"* because if you try to do otherwise you risk sounding very *"affected"* and fake. Remember, part of the magic of being a singer is delivering just who you are in a believable way. When it comes to vowel modification, your ears are your greatest learning tool.

Study different music styles and analyze what it is different singers do with their vowels and their consonants, as well as the relationship between these sounds. Experiment with your own songs, changing mouth shape and modifying sounds to see what feels right for you as a singer and right for the style of the song.

Refer to video tutorial **"Vowel Modification"**

VIBRATO-O-O-O-O-O

Tricky little thing, vibrato – it doesn't always come naturally to a singer. In your journey of developing good vocal technique, vibrato will surface – sometimes when you least expect it. What exactly is vibrato? Webster's Dictionary defines vibrato as *"a slightly tremulous effect imparted to vocal or instrumental tone for added warmth and expressiveness by slight and rapid variations in pitch."* What the heck does that mean? Well, to me it means being able to create a wave-like pattern in your voice when singing that fluctuates slightly above and below the perfect pitch of a note in order to add inflection or an emotional nuance. Besides using this effect for purposes of inflection or nuance, vibrato can play a more practical role in your performance, too. As you may already know, it is quite difficult to sing a straight note with absolute perfect pitch, so learning to use vibrato to approximate the note is a valuable skill for singers to acquire. How to create that waver is the mystery we are about to explore in the following paragraphs.

Vibrato and Diaphragm Support

When I teach something to my students I always sing it myself, paying close attention to what is happening with my body and voice. To me, vibrato is a phenomenon that is a blend of two physical experiences.
The first place I feel the vibrato control coming from is my diaphragm. You have to have correct movement of the breath, air in your tank and proper diaphragm engagement to help vibrato evolve. You will become aware of the diaphragm's support of vibrato once you start manipulating the vocal cords to help create it.

Vibrato And Vocal Cords

The second place I feel vibrato coming from is my throat… yes I said throat. After all the finger wagging in past chapters about staying out of your throat, I am giving you permission to engage a little throat movement. More specifically, I am giving you permission to engage your throat muscles slightly so you can open and close your vocal cords, creating the oscillating feeling of vibrato. Once you start this gentle muscle manipulation, you become more aware of your diaphragm support and its role in creating vibrato, as the vocal cord movement acts like a door opening and shutting off the breath flow from the diaphragm. It is these two actions that create a singer's vibrato.

Vibrato Exercise 1 – Half-Step Oscillation

This exercise is a great way to get the feel and control of vibrato if you have been unaware of it up to this point. Pay particular attention to what your diaphragm support and throat are doing during the process. Remember that diaphragm support only works when you have enough air in your tank.

a) In your mid-range, choose two notes a half-step or semi-tone apart. *(C-C#, for example)*

b) Using a metronome to keep time is a great idea, so go to *www.metronomeonline.com* and set it to 84 beats per minute, alternating the notes sung on "AH" with each "tick" and "tock" of the metronome *(e.g., tick-C /tock-C#).* Take a breath to fill up your tank so that you can start engaging slow and fluid diaphragm support, then slowly switch between the semi-tones on the vowel sound "AH" until your air gets depleted. You should only be able to do three or four pattern switches between the notes.

c) Repeat the above exercise, dividing the time in half by doing a complete pattern switch on a tick and a complete pattern switch on a tock *(e.g., tick-C-C#/tock-C-C#).*
At this point in the exercise I feel the resonance of notes high in my oral cavity.

d) Slow the metronome down to 60 beats per minute and sing two switching patterns between the tick and the tock *(e.g., tick-C-C#-C-C#/tock-C-C#-C-C#),* becoming aware of lowering the note resonance towards the back of your lower oral cavity *(yes, I mean throat – I hate it when I have to contradict myself).* Think of the tick and tock as the "1" of a 4-beat bar. You can even think "1-2-3-4" as you sing a note per beat. At this point, the size of the waver is still quite large as shown in *Figure 1.*

Figure 1. Half-Step Oscillation

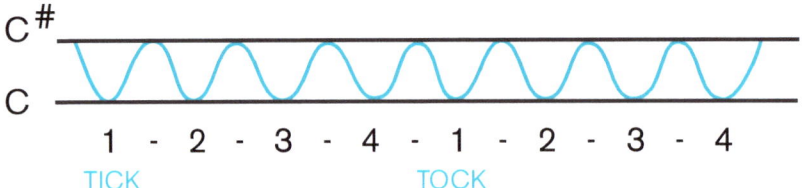

e) For the last part of this exercise, change the metronome marking to *72 beats per minute.* Take in a breath, engage your diaphragm support and think about lessening the size of the waver from a full semi-tone to only a slight variation of pitch on one note *(e.g., the C),* staying low in your oral cavity and manipulating the vocal cords to open and shut gently. Aim for *4 oscillations* on each tick and tock.

Be patient: once the oscillations kicks in with even cycles and feel natural, you've just found your vibrato.

Figure 2 - Vibrato on *"C"*

TICK   TOCK

Examples of Vibrato

In my world, there is no right or wrong vibrato – the secret lies with where and when you use it. Singers develop a natural vibrato that often becomes part of their signature sound. Let me give you some examples of different kinds of vibratos, all of which can be easily heard online *(thank goodness for YouTube!).* While these examples may not be from the most current roster of artists, they give insight into the range of possibilities that exists.

Slow and Wide Vibrato

Willie Nelson and *Robert Goulet* are two popular music singers in music history that have vibratos so wide you could throw a cat through them *(I heard that expression once and laughed so hard that I just had to put it in this manual).* Okay, their vibratos might not be that wide, but they definitely are on the slower and wider side, helping to make the comparison between vibrato styles. A little aside about slower vibrato – don't confuse it with a tremolo effect, which is a fluctuation of volume that mimics the cycles of slow sounding vibrato and is not actually a pitch waver but a volume fluctuation *(Aaron Neville sings with tremolo).* This is created solely from diaphragm support.

Fast and Narrow Vibrato

If you are familiar with 80s pop music, Belinda Carlisle has a machine gun rapid-fire vibrato that became her signature sound. Upon listening to her vibrato, you couldn't even insert a slip of paper between the wavers let alone a cat. It's fast. Dynamo Dolly Parton has a very fast vibrato lending itself well to her country and western style. Johnny Mathis, a popular singer in the late 50s and 60s, has a fairly fast and dominant vibrato that is the identifying characteristic of his voice. No mistaking that it's him - ever.

Minimal Vibrato

Every so often you hear a singer who has such a unique sound that it is hard to put your finger on why they sound so different. This was the case for me when I heard the incredibly sensual vocal style of Sade (another artist from the 80s and 90s.) When analyzing why her voice was so hypnotic, I realized she sings quite "straight" with little vibrato. Maintaining great pitch with minimal vibrato is a hard thing to do and thus an impressive feat. It becomes even more impressive, however, when we consider Sade recorded all her songs in an era when singers actually had to know how to sing and did not have their sound digitally manipulated or even manufactured in the studio as often is the case today. (Don't get me started on that!)

Vibrato Control

If you have listened to the examples mentioned above of the different artists' vibratos, you have probably noticed that you may favour one vibrato style over another. Learning to emulate all styles of vibrato is extremely useful when you do studio work and the producer requests a different vibrato, or when you want to mimic a particular musical style's vibrato.

Most singers have a natural, easy vibrato that you may not even notice. But if your natural vibrato tends to lean to one extreme or the other – "machine gun rapid-fire-fast" or "throw a cat through it slow" (LOL) – it may work against you, especially if you don't know how to control it. Vibrato control is particularly important when singing with others. To better understand why, visualize vibrato as a series of sound waves. If one singer has a slower, wider wave and the other has a faster, more frequent wave, the peaks and valleys won't necessarily line up at the same time. The result? Vibratos that compete as shown in Figure 3.

Figure 3 - Competing Vibratos

Once you are able to match another singer's vibrato, synchronization happens that sounds so much more fluid and professional.

Figure 4 - Matching Vibratos

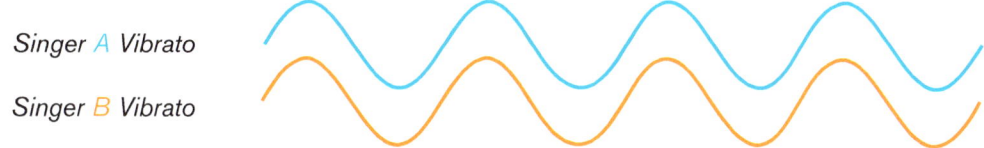

Once you have control of your vibrato, there are so many options of how to use it. Remember, however, that having this control doesn't mean every time you engage a note you add vibrato - quite the contrary. Often a **"less is more"** approach is most effective. Vibrato is like a nice seasoning in a recipe: if you use too much of it, the fine balance of your creation may be thrown off. Tasteful vibrato, then, might simply involve holding a note out with pure pitch before adding a few wavers of vibrato towards the end of the note's duration. *(Figure 5)*

Figure 5 - Less is More

Don't Get Frustrated - My Vibrato Story

When I was in a high school rock band many moons ago, I had a brilliant teacher who sent me home with a copy of The Hometown Band's song "Fear Of Flying" so I could listen to the lead singer's beautiful slow and soulful vibrato and emulate it. I studied the song all weekend and still couldn't seem to get a handle on it. In my frustration, I had to just "let it go" and forget about it. At the next band practice I started singing, and all of a sudden out came this fabulous vibrato that I had never used before – it just crept into my body and surfaced when it decided it was time. Years later that beautiful soulful singer, Shari Ulrich, handed me my Juno Award. It was a great night as I had been a huge fan of hers for years. We had a laugh later when I told my vibrato story. The point I want to make is that vibrato will show up eventually – just be aware of it and keep working at it.

Just to let you know, too, that as lovely as my first vibrato style was, I later subconsciously developed a chipmunk-like, super-fast vibrato that I have had to harness over the years. This experience has taught me to always be aware of my vibrato style and my control of it. Recording yourself singing at every opportunity is the best way to learn a lot about your personal vibrato style, as what you may hear in your head and what is actually happening can sometimes be two different things.

Summary

In summary, start paying attention to all your favourite singers' use of vibrato. See if you can emulate what they are doing, but be patient with yourself. Your personal vibrato will eventually appear, as mine did.
Once it does appear, experiment with it to decide how much, where and when to use it to make your song sound the best it can be. *(But don't forget about all the other POINTS too!)*

Photo by Dexter Quinto
theyrep.com

"Casa Do Samba" Album Cover

In the Studio Mapping Out Lyrics
Photo by Ken Stewart

MAPPING OUT YOUR LYRICS – REVISITED

As mentioned in **POINT 1 - BREATHING, POINT 2 - DIAPHRAGM SUPPORT,** and **POINT 5 - VOWEL MODIFICATION,** mapping out your lyrics is an essential tool in learning your song quickly and effectively for performance. By *"mapping out"* the lyrics, I mean creating a *"road map"* of where you need to breathe, engage your diaphragm, add trills, colour words, open vowels, clip words and notate the melody's direction. When learning a cover song, listening to the original reference while mapping out the song is a huge help.

Doing so allows you to hear where the singer is breathing, supporting with their diaphragm, trilling, and so on.

Breathmarks

As was discussed in **POINT 1 - BREATHING,** where you breathe and your breath size per phrase are very important in the performance of a song. This is called the breathing rhythm of the song. When I am preparing a song for performance, I identify its unique breathing rhythm by putting check marks on the lyric sheet where I need to take a breath. If I know I need a larger breath, I will darken the check mark. You may choose to use other symbols as your breathmarks, but it is important to define where breaths are needed and to identify breaths needing to be more substantial. This is the first and most important step in mapping out your lyrics.

If the breathing rhythm of the song is not correct, nothing else will work well and the delivery of the song will feel like a ride down a bumpy road. Ultimately, breathing correctly is important for good pitch and power and to create a natural fluidity to the delivery of the song.

Diaphragm Support

Identifying where you need to engage your diaphragm and how much of it you need is the second most important step in mapping out your lyrics. Typically, you need to start adding diaphragm support when you are singing notes in your mid range and above. For instance, when you have to sing a note in your *Diva/Rockstar Placement,* you will be using major diaphragm support. We learned in **POINT 2** that I like to call this type of diaphragm support *"calling voice."* To better understand this, pretend to "call" to someone across the street, all the while paying attention to what your breathing/diaphragm support is doing. You will most likely be taking in a very large singer's breath and then pulling your diaphragm quickly towards your backbone, projecting the sound out with power. On my lyric sheet, I put a crescendo symbol (<) underneath the words or syllables where I need to engage my diaphragm. The more support I need, the darker I make the symbol.

The actual physical diaphragm "pull" towards your backbone will feel like a small pulse all the way to a larger pull depending on what range you are in and how much support you will need on that particular word or syllable.

Trills

Trills are the groups of notes that typically extend off the end of a word or are part of an "ad–lib" or "made-up" phrase. Some will ascend melodically and some will descend. If there is a three-note trill that descends melodically off a word, I write a symbol of three descending steps. If the trill ascends, I note three ascending steps. If it is a five-note trill, I do the same with the correct number of steps per note.

With trills, it is also very important to hit each note precisely and not just gliss, or slide over it, which sounds messy and amateur. Pay attention to how the notes are grouped rhythmically, too, as this will make them sound groovy or square in the delivery of the trill. If you sing the notes all even rhythmically and too "on the beat" they will sound square with no "feel" to them. If you notice that maybe the first and second notes are grouped together, then the third note is elongated and the fourth and fifth notes are grouped together, then you will be able to duplicate the pitch and "feel" of the trill, making it sound really "pro."

Every trill will be different. Slow each down until you get precision in the number of notes, pitch and rhythm and then sing it at the right tempo when you know how to do it correctly.

Colour Words

There are certain words that beg to be "coloured" in the performance of the song. By this I mean adding inflection *(a growl, emotional tone or more air around the tone of your voice)* to make the song's delivery more distinctive. Part of performing a song well is singing it with emotion, preventing the song from sounding boring and one-dimensional. Colouring words and adding dynamics *(louds and softs)* will help infuse emotion in a song.

Modifying or Opening Vowels

We've already talked at length about **POINT 5 - VOWEL MODIFICATION.** To re-cap it is important as you ascend in your vocal range to open up your vowels by dropping your jaw in order for the words to float out with effortlessness and not be tight or "squeezy." This is especially true when you are in your Diva/Rockstar Placement engaging a lot of diaphragm support. When mapping out the lyrics for a song, I will put a semi-circular arrow over the word or syllable of a word that needs to be opened. Often, I will also write a word and how to modify the vowels in the margin of the lyric sheet. For example, "I" = "AHy." I opened the vowel on the word "I" by hanging on the "AH" sound and closing at the very last moment with a tiny "y" *(EE)* sound.

Vowel sounds that always need to be opened include any with the "EE" sound which you modify to an "EH" *(as in, "I'm Canadian, EH")* formation of the mouth but still sing an "EE" sound.

As we have already discussed in **POINT 5** it's a little strange as you think "EH," but still sing "EE." You will be amazed at how this makes the delivery of a word so much more open and easier to hit pitch-wise in the higher ranges of your voice. Have your radar on for any words that feel a bit tight to sing in the higher range of your voice and be aware of dropping the jaw to open up the vowel, making it easier to sing. This approach can be adjusted to work for many different vowel sounds.

Clipping Words

Often we tend to hang onto a word too long which will cover up a natural space to breathe in the song. As breathing is the most important part of mapping out your lyrics, I often coach people to "clip" some of the words shorter to create a space for a breath mark. It often helps the phrasing of a pop song by clipping the words, too. If you tend to hold your words or phrases too long you can take the song out of a pop style and move it more towards a musical theatre or classical sounding style. The same is true if you default to the lighter Mask Area placement when you should be staying in Diva/Rockstar placement. Staying true to the groove and the intent of the song is very important. Keeping your words and phrases shorter not only enables you to put all the breath marks in the right spots, but it also ultimately has a big impact on the emotional delivery of the song.

Notating Direction Of The Melody

When I have to learn a song quickly, I often use arrows up or down above certain words to remind me that the melody is going to take significant "jump" in that direction. You will be amazed at how well your "ear" will work to take you to the correct note when you have given your brain a little help by adding the arrow.

Train Your Brain

Once you have your lyric sheet mapped out, use it while you are practising your song. After a few passes, your brain will start to absorb all the things you need to do in order to perform the song in a technically correct way. Then you will be able to remove the lyric sheet and just sing the song. My motto is "think about it for a while and then just forget about it and sing the darn song." You will get to a point where you will recognize where you missed a breath or a diaphragm pull or where you needed to open up a tight vowel sound by modifying it. Also, try to anticipate what is coming next in your vocal map so you are ready for it when you get there and not when you are passing over it.

Mapping Out - Exercise 1

Do a fully mapped out lyric sheet with all of the above-mentioned techniques to create the road map to follow as you sing the song.

Refer to video tutorial "Mapping Out Your Lyrics"

*Angela & Her Dear Friend Catherine St. Germain
Singing with the Polyester Philharmonic
Photo by Ken Stewart*

MICROPHONE TECHNIQUE FOR LIVE PERFORMANCE

There are some basic guidelines for singing into a "stage" microphone. **First, repeat after me:** "I am not afraid of the microphone." When used correctly, the microphone can be your best friend. You will use a slightly different approach on the microphone with each range of your voice. Your goal is to get the best warmth, body and tonal nuances of your voice to project through the microphone. Oh yeah, and always say "check" into a mic when testing it. Don't blow into it...bad form.

Low-Range (Chest Voice/Placement)

Generally speaking, when you are singing in your low- range (chest voice) and your ultra low-range, you want to be right up "on" the microphone (Figure 1) Your lips may even make contact to get the best "read" of the notes you are singing. Of course, you want to do this on a freshly cleaned mic or your own personal one. (I always carry a small bottle of antibacterial mouthwash and cosmetic pads for cleaning communal mics before I use them). As this range is not often the most powerful in a person's voice, you will not want to wander more than a centimetre or half an inch away.

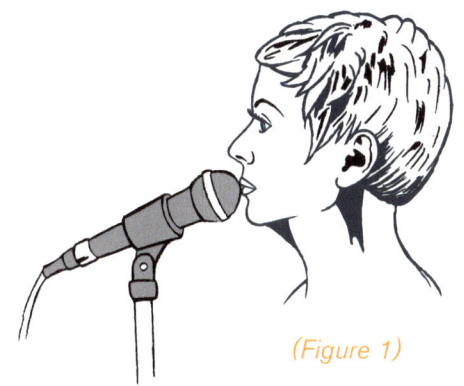

(Figure 1)

Mid-Range (Full Voice/Speaking Tonality Placement)

In your mid-range with medium volume projection you will want to be 2–5 centimetres (1 to 2 inches) away from the mic (Figure 2) This range of our voice "cuts" a little better and you do not need to cuddle up too close to the mic or your power will make the part of the mic called "the diaphragm" over-vibrate and cause distortion. Zeroing in on what is coming out of the sound system will help you gauge how far you can wander off the mic. If your voice suddenly sounds thin or tinny, you know that you have come off the mic too far.

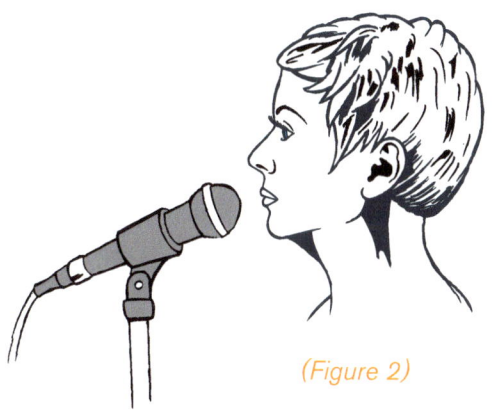

(Figure 2)

Upper-Mid-Range
(Diva/Rockstar Placement)

The moment you feel that *Whitney Houston, Celine Dion, Janis Joplin, Freddy Mercury, Jon Bon Jovi or Mike Reno* have entered your body and you are going for the big notes, make sure you pull away from your mic about 10 to 15 cm *(4 to 6 inches or for fingers away) (Figure 3)*

This is a super powerful range, and you want to avoid distortion or taking your audience's heads off with too much volume. Again, try to hear what is coming out of the sound system to help you gauge your distance.

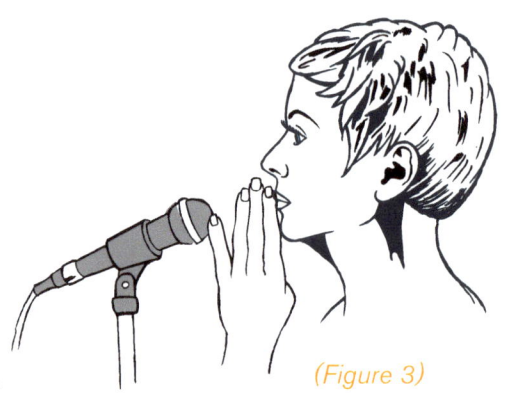

(Figure 3)

Higher – Lighter Range
(Mask Area Placement)

Once you flip up into your mask area resonance, you will want to return to the mid-range approach of 2-5 centimetres away. Sometimes I tell my students to think 2 fingers away *(Figure 4)*. As this resonance is lighter and airier, being too far off the mic will cause you to lose the ambience of your tone.

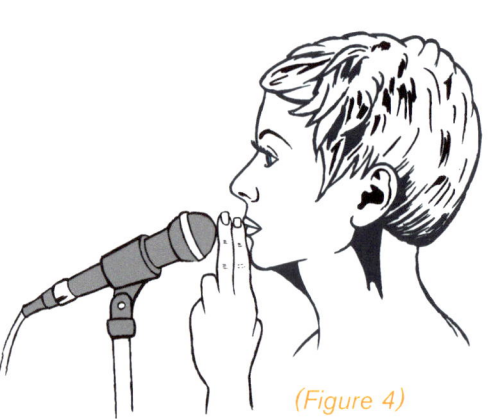

(Figure 4)

Higher – With Power
(Supermask Placement)

Remember when we talked about *Supermask Placement* in **POINT 3?** This is a variation of Mask Area placement with a different, more powerful diaphragm support. Because you are adding the power element in this range you will want to gauge your distance from the microphone accordingly judging by what you are hearing come out of the sound system. General rule of thumb would be to back away from the mic about 5 centimetres.

Microphone Positioning

When using a microphone, the angles of both the microphone and your head are important in getting the best results both visually and audio-wise. *(Figure 5)* depicts the correct angle of both the microphone and your head.

Note that the angle of the microphone does not in anyway obstruct the view of the face and is angled downward. Also, note the chin is parallel to the floor and the microphone is centred between the nose and the chin.

Figure 5

In Figure 6, the chin is too low and will create problems in this position: a double chin *(bad)* and a closure of your airway. This won't work when trying to sing the open floaty notes we aim for as singers.

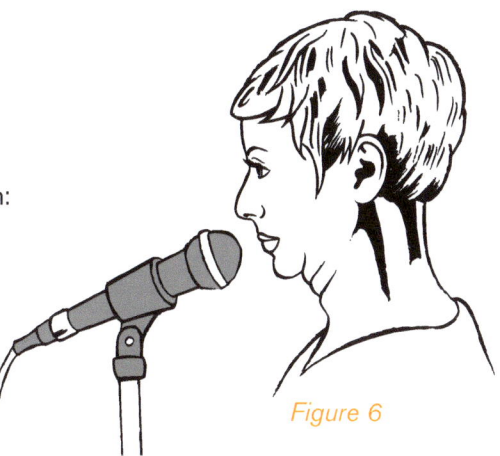

Figure 6

The last illustration *(Figure 7)* portrays the opposite of the double chin/air obstructing illustration. The chin position is far too high creating tightness in the throat area making it difficult to sing the open floaty notes once again.

Figure 7

Keep in mind that these depictions are general guidelines. Once you know your voice and develop good microphone technique you can push the boundaries a little for dramatic effect if needed while performing. You will be able to recognize if a certain action makes it more difficult to sing with ease and adjust the position accordingly.

Finding The Right Microphone

Once again, there are exceptions to every rule. Use your ears to help develop your personal microphone technique. Also, every microphone has different sensitivities and is set up to favour certain frequencies. You want to get the best overall "fullness" for your voice out of your mic. For fun, go into a music store like **Long & McQuade** or **Tom Lee** here in Canada and experiment with different microphones in the store's mic studio, paying attention to which ones make your voice sound the best. You may be surprised how great the differences can be from one mic to the next. FYI, recording studio microphones are much more sensitive and require a different approach that we will discuss in the STUDIO SINGING chapter.

Refer to video tutorial "Microphone Technique"

Angela on Stage with Farmer's Daughter

STAGE PERFORMANCE TIPS

It's pretty much assumed that you are a capable singer if you get to the point where you are taking the stage, but I am often a little surprised at how intimidated some singers can be when it comes to their performance. At this point, I'd like to share some of my favourite *"dos and don'ts"* to give you some ideas on how to make your overall performance look and feel more professional. Remember, while these are guidelines and personal preferences, I think you'll find they represent *"common performance sense."*

Microphone Stands

Let's start with microphone stands. I have a major pet peeve when it comes to the use of microphone stands. *Let me tell you about it…*

If you are not using your microphone stand, put it behind you. Put it far enough away that you won't trip on it. Resist the urge to take the mic off the stand and then play with the stand, unless it's part of your act. Removing it from the front line will create a clear visual path for photo opportunities and give the audience an unobstructed view of your performance. Sometimes, something as subtle as leaving an unused microphone stand in front of you creates a psychological barrier between you and your audience. You want to project the feeling of including your audience in your performance and leaving an unused stand in front of you doesn't extend that invitation. It may even seem that you are hiding behind it. Be aware of not putting it in front of anyone else on stage as well *(that's how divas are born).*

Songs, Keys and Tempos

Another tip to help you be more professional is to know the key your song is in and the tempo. Always have a *"standard"* *(a song that every band should know)* in your back pocket in case you find yourself somewhere where you can get up and sing with a band. To give the right tempo, sing a line or two where you like it so the musician counting in the song can feel the beat and bring in the rest of the band accordingly. Additionally, learn some musical lingo so you can communicate to the musicians and not sound like a dumb singer…sometimes we are viewed as the lowest beings in the musical food chain. Knowing some appropriate lingo is a sure way to gain respect quickly.

Composing A Set List

There is a certain energy that you want to create when assembling the list of your songs for performance. Personally, I would never start or end a set list with a ballad. You may have one in mind that is musically brilliant and emotionally moving, but ballads generally have a unique energy that should be placed strategically in the set. I will often place a ballad about 3/4 of the way into a set, just as the performance is building energy to add a shot of intensity. I then close the set with a few more energetic songs.

Opening with something that really grabs the audience's attention is always a good way to set the tone for the performance: the same applies to the last song of the set. You want to leave the stage with something that has the right energy, as that is most likely what your audience will remember most. I like to think of a set list as an emotional rollercoaster ride: it might start off with a burst of energy, then it might take a curve, then it goes even higher and faster, then it might dip into a valley for a different or intense kind of energy, then it builds again before coming into the station. You will get a feel for what works and how well the songs might group together the more you perform. In addition, sometimes it works well to have songs that have a similar tempo or are in the same or a complimentary key follow one another so that you can easily or cleverly transition from one into the next. That's called a *"segue"* and adds interest for the listener *(instead of just hearing one song after another with a break in between.)*

No matter how you plan your set, you want to make the set list feel like a journey to keep the show stimulating for both the audience and the band.

Connecting With Your Audience

I am hoping that by the time you get to perform on a stage you will feel very confident with your songs and the way you sing or play your instrument. There is, however, the dreaded *"talking to the audience before songs"* banter, which can be quite frightening for some performers. If the idea of such banter makes you nervous, **RELAX** – it's not as scary as it might seem. Generally, telling stories of how you wrote a particular song or why you chose another works well, but that approach might get a little old after about the third number.

So, how do you make the banter interesting and entertaining?

In my experience, I have found that including your audience in different ways is a major step to making a great connection and having them feel like they are a part of the show. What I mean by this is don't be afraid to ask a question of the audience and respond directly to some of the answers you might get.

There might be a guy who thinks he's funny and you can have an ongoing rapport with him for the rest of the performance that can be tasteful and humorous. Or, sometimes it can be fun to have the audience sing along or shout out a part at a strategic time to help create a party-like atmosphere if that is the kind of show you put on. Training your audience to sing a part will work especially well if they have seen or heard your music before. However, be aware that sometimes an audience doesn't want to play your games. Read the crowd and you will know when and if you can get some participation out of them. If something works well once, chances are it will work well again and you may want to incorporate it into every show. What happens as a reaction to something or happens spontaneously can also easily become part of your performance banter for all your shows.

Sometimes it just takes a little research into who and where your audience is to give you ideas of what to talk about between the tunes and ultimately make a connection. For instance, you might consider finding funny, local facts that the audience already knows about and bringing these up: an approach I can personally vouch for. One time I was in a town where I heard the local news proclaiming that they had just been given the honour of being the car theft capital of Canada. *(I found that funny…use your own discretion).*
That night at the show, I worked that into the banter. It was funny and fun and people were impressed that I knew something *(even if it wasn't that flattering of a statistic)* about their town. Having and using your sense of humour makes information like that go over well and allows you to win over the audience with your wit and personality in addition to your musical talent.

I always feel that it's a great thing to acknowledge the people who help your show be a success.
It is important that if you have crew working with you, for instance, to give them credit. The crew are the ones who help load your gear, do the sound or lights and manage many of the other duties needed to put on a great show. They are in fact often the unsung heroes of this business. They are the first people there, the last to leave and have the success of the way you sound and the way you look at their fingertips. Incorporating an acknowledgement and thanks to the crew somewhere in your show is very classy and impressive. You will be amazed at how such a simple acknowledgement will also make people want to bend over backwards for you the next time you work together. Similarly, if you are playing in a bar where there are bartenders and wait staff, recognize them, thank them for working so hard for the patrons, encourage big tips and make them feel that they are a part of the success of the night as well. All in all, remember that it takes a team to put on a great performance, so show your appreciation for everyone who contributes.

R.E.S.P.E.C.T On Stage

Playing in a band is such a fun and fulfilling experience. It's really important to recognize that it's a team effort and give each other the spotlight. As a singer, especially a lead singer, you might be the focus of attention for most of the performance. Before all you musicians and side guys start sending me hate mail, let me explain. I think that because everyone has a voice and tries to sing at one point or another in their lives, everyone automatically relates to the singer. If you are a guitar player or drummer, you may focus on that musician for most of the night, but most people relate first to the singer. So, my advice to all singers out there who want to share the privilege of having the audience's attention is the following. First, when a musician is taking a solo, turn in their direction to pull the audience's focus toward them. Next, never speak over a solo; give the soloing player or singer the respect of your attention and everyone else's. Finally, encourage the audience to clap after a brilliant solo. I feel that some audiences have become quite lazy in their responses over the years. I'm therefore on a mission to teach people how to respond to a fabulous performance and give credit where credit is due. Working as a team by showing each other respect gives a sense of cohesiveness and professionalism to the performance. Check your ego at the door. It's not attractive to see a battle of egos on stage.

Stage Attire

It is my humble opinion that being on stage is a privilege. It's a special occasion, a celebration of being able to do what we do as singers and musicians. Dress for that occasion. I get that some bands like to be just who they are and not get too fussed about what they look like, but I like to see performers who put some effort into what they wear on stage, to interviews, public appearances, and so on. I really believe that dressing well will take you up a notch in the esteem of your audience, too.

Fashion and the music business have always gone hand in hand. That said, fashion and style don't have to cost a fortune. *(As outlined in the the next chapter "Jake's Fashion/Style Philosophy".)*

There are many ways and places to find your stage style and start creating an image if you don't already have one – it's part of the fun of the journey of making great music. If you want to wear the same clothes that you poured concrete in or went to the gym in earlier that day, that's up to you, but I think deep down, we all want to show off our inner Divas and Rockstars, which will only enhance our performances.

While it's important to keep all these tips in mind, what's most important is just get out there to sing and perform as much as possible. You will learn more from that school of hard-knocks than from anything else.

Enjoy the journey!

Farmer's Daughter Make Up Artist Gina Hole Lazarowich on Video Set with Angela.

Photo by Ken Stewart

Farmer's Daughter Promo Photo 1998
Photo by Barry Gnyp

JAKE'S FASHION AND STYLE PHILOSPHY

My philosophy when it comes to fashion and style is simple. **LOOK FABULOUS!!**

THE END!

Oh…you want details. Looking fabulous doesn't mean you have to follow the current runway trends to a T, or break the bank! It does mean finding what works for you, whatever your body type, including all figure fla…nope, won't say it – figure *"rarities."* Much better! It means finding a realistic, artistic approach to dressing your body. It has to make sense to you, your personality, lifestyle, career and your genetic makeup, baby! It means understanding fully what you like and why. Knowing what makes you feel great, what looks amazing and how to put a spin on what you're wearing which represents your brain and in your case…. your music! *Confidence is key* in this *"biz,"* and when you feel great about your appearance, it shows. Never underestimate the value of developing your look and being consistent with your brand.

I've received a diploma in fashion merchandising. I've worked as a model, performer and stylist. Having experience in each of these facets of the industry has allowed me to look at the process of clothing *(verb)* from different angles. My experience has taught me what is required to create a street and stage look designed to bring you confidence and set you apart…in a good way.

In this wee overview I want to give you a few things to think about *(maybe 5 – that seems to be a respectable number).* These are items that would be topic of conversation for us if we were beginning a styling session in real time.

Don't confuse fashion with style!

Fashion is a beautiful thing and we use elements of it to create style. Fashion is dictated by the powers that be *(e.g., design houses)* and conformed to by the people *(that would be us).* Fashion is timely, and that's why you can be in or out of "it." In fashion, the story is about the clothing.

Style is what we get when we study fashion, take what we love from it and mix it with eclectic parts of our existing wardrobe – perhaps a vintage piece or something you love from last season/decade. You, as a musician are a character, not a clothes-hanger. Style can be loaded with or merely have hints of current trends. Therefore, there's no expiry date. *In style, the story is about you!*

Know *(and love)* your *body!* This is a very extensive section that I will try to make as simple as possible. Take a scan of yourself top to bottom: the eye responds to relative balance. So simply put, if something seems in great disproportion to the next, think *"balance".* I will demonstrate with an example: let's say you have an absolutely *huuuuuuge* ...Adam's apple. You may want to consider a substantial hairstyle or a strong hat. We don't hide...we balance. Now, scan on down the rest of your beautiful self and repeat the exercise.

Understand the vibe of your music, what is expected of you on stage, and your audience.

RESPECT ALL THREE!

a) The vibe of your music. *What do you sing about? What is your instrumentation? What does your music say?* What do you talk about in between songs? How does this all look to an audience? If you're singing about your neighbours and church picnics, the black leather dog collar around your neck with the spikes paired with black lipstick and nail polish *(I'm talking to both sexes, here)* probably won't get you that encore you're looking for. If you are a young girl singing about boys, love, mom, friends, guitars, tears and dreamy things (huge sigh), then that flowery, colourful, sundress with cowboy boots is perfect.

b) Understand what is expected of you on stage physically. If you're an active performer and have vigorous gestures, make sure your clothing allows you to go for it full on. There's enough to think about on stage other than making adjustments to your clothing. If you're the rock god who always has that one arm straight up to the heavens, that fabulous tight-sleeved Euro suit jacket will feel like a straightjacket.
If you love to stride from one side of the stage to the other, that slimming pencil skirt is going to turn you into a Geisha. Some things look great when you try them on but you've got to try them out! Make sure that you are able to do what you do *(including breathe)* in your chosen get-up. So, before you step out on the stage with something brand spankin' new, make sure you put it on and assume all possible manoeuvres to prevent your audience from feeling your pain – because they will.

c) Understand your audience. As a result of understanding the vibe of your music, you will know who will be listening to and buying it. *Be daring* but don't alienate the people who support you: they must see an element of themselves in you to feel the draw. You can say, *"forget it man, I'll wear what I want, I just gotta be me,"* but if the audience that your music targets doesn't understand at least part of what you have on you've **LOST THEM!** If your audience is counting on you to be over the top, then don't let them down. I'm not telling you to reel it in or sell out. I'm telling you to be smart and incredibly observant: **KNOW YOUR AUDIENCE AND DELIVER!**

Never be afraid to **TRY!** Don't shut something down before you give it a life! Don't be that person who says, *"No, that would never work on me,"* or *"Oh, I'm sure that wouldn't look right or go together."* Some of my greatest success stories have been the result of a simple, *"I know it sounds crazy, but let's just TRY it."* Opposing patterns, colours that don't seem to be an obvious combination, juxtaposition of style…*just TRY!* If I had a pair of shoes for every client who said *"you've got to be kidding me,"* and then promptly fell in love with their new look…oh, wait a minute – I do. Ha! Seriously, trying out new or unconventional looks is how you take a straight-forward fashion statement and turn it into something unique and meaningful.

Stick to your brand! Now that you understand the 4 suggestions above and have some pointers on how to think about your personal style, stick to it. Your style is your brand, and it's how people see and identify you. When you switch it up too often there's nothing to recognize! If your audience can't recognize you from one appearance to another it's not a look but a disguise. I don't think I need to elaborate on the dangers of your audience not recognizing you from week to week!

My love affair with fashion/style is tied strongly to a sense of humour, which I believe is imperative when speaking of our ever-evolving fashion/style world. Always be aware of the current trends, but use them as a frame to infuse your own spirit. Don't be afraid to look at that vintage suit from Value Village and say, *"That would be a knock-out with a starchy white French cuff blouse,"* then rock it out with more chains than a motorcycle gang in the 70s. You see, it's all in how we pair items – it's the old mixed with the new, it's the expensive mixed with the bargain variety, it's the eccentric wild-child piece married to the conservative element. It's all of the above or one single element that creates unique style and allows us in our daily street lives and in our performance mode to achieve true *"flare."* And remember, it's all garbage without a confident smile, a sincere laugh, and a firm handshake. **ROCK ON!**

*Farmer's Daughter and Randy Bachman
Recording the BTO cover "Let It Ride"
Photo by Ken Stewart*

STUDIO SINGING

Singing in the recording studio is a totally different animal than performing live. In a live show, if you hit a "funky" *(as in, "not good")* note, it passes into the atmosphere never to be heard again.

In the recording studio, if you hit a funky note it will forever be burned into the track for everyone to enjoy over and over and over again. Thus, before you set foot into a studio, it is important to know what you are doing through good vocal technique to ensure you don't waste your money and your time. What better reason than to study "The 5 Point Singing System" first! *(Is that school-marm, lecturing thing happening again?)*

To give you a bit more insight into the studio, here are some terms used when recording to help you communicate and speak the same language as the people you will be creating with.

Studio Vocabulary

STUDIO - A space that is used to record music or voice productions. Often it will have a myriad of instruments to be used within it. There may also be smaller, isolated rooms used for recording individual instruments or voices.

PRODUCER - *The "Head Honcho"* or *"Grand Poobah"* of the session. What a director is to a movie, the producer is to the session. He/She is the person you hire to create magic out of your songs and get the best out of you vocally.

ENGINEER - This person is the technical wizard you hire to get all the "sounds": he/she tweaks all the levels and effects to make you and the track sound the best. The engineer works hand in hand with the producer and is usually the producer's second in command.

CONTROL ROOM - This is the space where all the recording gadgetry is. It is "command central" for the producer and engineer.

SESSION - The session refers to the time you spend in the studio on any given day.

HEADPHONES - Also known as "cans" or "phones." There is a left side and a right side, so look for the corresponding letter on each side. You wear them to create isolation of sound and will hear your voice and all the music through them rather than a speaker.

TRACK - The music you hear in your headphones, which is a combination of all the instruments together. The term "track" also refers to an individual part of the big picture *(e.g., "the guitar track" or "the vocal track")*.

MIX - The balance of instruments, vocals and effects in your headphones or on the track.

REVERB - A type of effect that a producer or engineer may add to your vocal to soften the edges a little. Also know as "verb." There are many effects that can be created in the studio but reverb is predominantly used when recording vocals.

TAKE - A "pass" of the song that will be recorded *(e.g.,"let's do a take")*. A "pass" may mean the same thing or just be a practise run of the song without recording. Make sure you distinguish between the two with your producer and engineer first as you don't want to sing the best vocal of your life and find out later that it was just an unrecorded practise run.

ISOLATION BOOTH - Also known as the "iso booth." This is a soundproof room typically found within a studio used to "isolate" sounds during a recording session, preventing bleed-through of other instrument noise onto another track. Iso booths are often used for recording drums and vocals.

CLIENT - A term often used in the advertising business to describe the person purchasing the promotional ditties known as "jingles." The client will usually be in the studio when the jingle is recorded. This can be unnerving, but know your stuff as well as you can and breathe, breathe, breathe. It will all turn out fine.

Studio Etiquette - Gear

It is a good habit NEVER to touch any of the equipment in the studio. For instance, if your microphone is at the wrong height, ask the engineer or the assistant engineer to adjust it for you: usually they are aware of your needs before you have to ask. The gear in the studio is worth a fortune and you don't want to be the one to drop it.

Getting What You Want In Your Mix

Don't be afraid to ask for adjustments in your mix to achieve a better balance of vocals, tracks and effects in your headphones. It's really important to be comfortable with what you are hearing in your phones to get the best vocal track you can. Less reverb, more reverb, balance of vocals and individual instrument tracks are all part of personal taste and it's your prerogative to ask the engineer to tweak the mix until you are hearing what you want. For example, I always prefer to hear more of the piano and not too much reverb in my mix. This gives me the solid pitch reference I need to sing a great pass or take of the song.

Studio Microphone Technique

Microphone technique in the studio can be a bit different than live performance mic technique.
There are many similar principles of proper mic technique between live and studio performance, but generally, studio mics are much more expensive, sensitive and dynamic than live mics. Your producer will guide you as to how close to be to the mic in relation to what the overall production of the song needs vocally.
You will also learn to gauge your proximity to the mic by what emotional value you want to record the track with *(e.g., closer proximity would result in a more intimate breathy vocal sound…)* and by what you are hearing in your headphones. Finally, know that studio mics will distort more easily than live mics as they are much more sensitive and intimate-sounding. So, learn to work the mic at different proximities without losing any vocal magic, especially when you hit your more powerful Diva/Rockstar notes.

Troubleshooting Pitch Problems

As I mentioned earlier in *"Getting What You Want In Your Mix,"* you may have to adjust what you are hearing in your headphones to ensure good pitch. Perhaps bringing up a certain track in the mix *(like piano)* or lessening the dominance of another will help. Another trick that we studio singers use is to pull one of the "cans" *(one side of the headphones)* off one ear a little. Doing so allows you to hear a bit of the ambient sound in the room in conjunction with your natural voice.

Hydrate Hydrate Hydrate!

Try to avoid drinking excessive amounts of coffee or caffeinated drinks, alcohol, or high-sugar content beverages in the studio. Water is always the best option to keep your vocal cords and your brain hydrated and energized when spending long hours in the studio where you need to constantly perform.

AVOID dairy for a few hours before you sing, too, as it creates phlegm in your throat that is hard to clear. If you are having throat issues and it's your day to sing, caffeine-free herbal teas or hot water with honey and lemon are both very soothing.

The studio can be a magical place of creativity and artistic bonding with other musicians and singers. Don't be intimidated by it. Being prepared with good vocal technique and an understanding of the nuances of your voice will give you great confidence in this very cool and fascinating environment.

Angela's Friend, Shane Hendrickson
Bass Player for FD & Polyester Philharmonic
Photo by Ken Stewart

Angela & Farmer's Daughter Sound Check for the Mike Bullard Show

Back-Up Singing 101

Knowing how to sing back-up or background vocals ("BGs") is an important skill to acquire as a singer. Background singers can add musical energy to a performance both in sound and visual presentation. Learning the skills and understanding the role of a "BG" singer on stage or in the studio will open up more opportunities for you as a vocalist.

The Role of a "BG" Singer – Live Performance

Background singers are used to enhance a lead singer's vocal performance by providing harmonies and strengthening the overall vocal sound. A background singer's delivery should always support the lead singer's performance and not compete with it. Learning to blend your vocal with the lead singer and other BG singers is therefore an important skill. The following guidelines will help in the development of your background vocal expertise.

a) Make sure the volume on your microphone is not obnoxiously louder than any of the other singer's microphones, especially the lead singer's *(you won't get hired again).* If there is a sound technician, the vocal balance for the "front of house" sound should be their responsibility, but being too loud applies to volume in the stage monitors as well which are adjusted at your request. If you are working without a sound technician, proximity to the microphone can help you blend with the other singers.

When hearing yourself over and above others, pull off the microphone a little until you mix better into the overall sound and don't dominate. The opposite works as well. If you are not hearing enough of yourself in the vocal mix, either ask the sound technician for more of your microphone level in the monitor or get closer to the microphone. This is the first part of what it means to "blend" with the other singers regarding the level of your voice against theirs: when singing BGs, you need to use your ears as well as your voice.

The BG section ultimately needs to work as a team so that everyone is hearing what they need to hear in order to do the best job possible.

The Role of a "BG" Singer – Live Performance

b) The second part of getting a good blend in a BG section is to know how to create an airier sound of your voice. This can be achieved by letting more air seep out around your vocal tone. The air will come from your diaphragm support so it may mean pulling in your diaphragm more quickly to get that surge of air around the tone. Your air will deplete more quickly than normal when adding air to your tone, possibly changing your breathing rhythm by adding more breaths or the capacity of air that you take in with each breath. Remember all the information about "Air To Tone Ratio" in **POINT 2?** This is one instance where it will come into play.

c) Pay attention to the lead singer's vibrato – is it a fast vibrato, slow vibrato, no vibrato? Try to match styles so there isn't a competition of vibratos going on. Competing vibrato waves can cause pitch problems or "out of sync" sounds in the vocals, also known as "flanging" in musical terms.

d) Lastly, be prepared with your parts. Once hired to do a BG gig, get the reference material well ahead of time, ask what part(s) you will be singing, and study those parts. It is so much more impressive when a BG singer or musician shows up to the rehearsal or gig knowing exactly what they need to and are not trying to fake their way through because they haven't put in the time to learn the part yet. This is a waste of everyone's time and not very professional. While preparation is important, it sometimes may not be possible if parts are not designated until a rehearsal. If this is the case, using a handheld recording device to record your part while rehearsing is an exceptional tool in learning your part quickly with precision. I try to learn my parts like you would a melody - being strong and solid on it.

If you follow the above guidelines, you will get a great reputation for being reliable, professional and a great team player. These are the skills that will get you hired again and again.

Movement of the BG Singer - Live Performance

Once again, in a live performance situation, it is important to be a support to the lead singer and not a distraction vocally or visually. If you have ever seen a professional BG section at work, you will notice that they are often placed on one part of the stage and seldom move from that position. This doesn't mean they should stand there like scarecrows, however. An easy, gentle movement such as a small side-to-side step or some choreographed arm movements are usually the norm. These smaller movements may also change from song to song. Occasionally, BG singers are also dancers in a big stage production, but when they are not, minimal, non-distracting movements are the best professional approach to the performance. If the lead singer wants more movement or action from you, they will ask. Starting smaller is the best way to go.

BG Singing In The Studio

Being in the recording studio is one of my very favourite things to do. However, it can be intimidating for many people. As it is a much more controlled environment than that of live performance, every flubbed line or missed note is time wasted. In the recording studio time is money, whether it's your own or someone else's, so you will want to be as efficient as possible without losing any of the soul and accuracy of the vocal performance. Also, as mentioned earlier, we sometimes haven't heard the song we'll be adding the complimentary vocal to until we get to the studio, and that in itself can be terribly intimidating. In such a situation, there are a few things you can do to make sure you get the best vocal performance on the recording accurately, emotionally and efficiently.

a) Know your voice as well as all the nuances of your tone and how to control them. We've already talked about knowing how to manipulate your tone with air and controlling the vibrato. This is especially important when working with other singers. If you are the only singer singing all the parts, you will want to match your own tone and vibrato on each track to make the BG section sound great.

BG Singing In The Studio *Continued*

b) Remember that the producer is the "Grand Poobah" of the session and will give you a lot of direction as to how he/she would like the parts sung. As hired BG singers we take that direction and give producers what they want. Sometimes a producer will ask for input into how a part should be delivered, but unless asked, it's respectful to follow his or her direction. If it's your session and you are paying the studio tab, you can experiment with many different options, but remember, time is money *(that's the Scottish/Capricorn/Realist coming out in me.)*

c) When singing in a BG section, the producer and/or engineer will give you direction on how close to the microphone you need to be. While getting levels in the control room, they will give direction on where you should stand based on the blend of vocals they want to hear from the overall BG section, or your precise individual level if you are on your own track. Remember to let the engineer move the very expensive gear if it needs to be repositioned.

d) If you are learning a song for the first time in the studio, mapping out a lyric sheet so that you have what you need to do vocally right there in front of you will save a lot of time and frustration. It takes the pressure off having to remember everything you need to sing during the course of the song, as you will be able to see exactly what you need to do and where. For these reasons, I always have a music stand and pencil close to the microphone in order to map out the lyrics. I intentionally suggest a "pencil" because things often change as you are working through a song.

e) I have never been a fan of sitting down to sing when performing live or in studio. This is my personal preference and there are exceptions, but I just like to have my diaphragm "unscrunched" *(is that a word? It is now!)* when singing so that my breathing and diaphragm support work as efficiently as possible. For me, standing enables effortless, accurate singing which ultimately means good pitch and power.

f) BE ON TIME! You don't want to be the one holding up the session or performance. This kind of behaviour sticks in people's minds for years, and you don't want that reputation. Showing respect for everyone's time as well as the studio time is very important when working in this environment.

Becoming a reputable BG singer may take a little time, but enjoy the journey: your confidence level will increase with every gig, and you'll work with and learn from some great singers along the way.

As you take this journey, also keep in mind that much of this business is referral from other singers and musicians. Following the guidelines outlined in this segment will help you establish a great reputation for being reliable, professional and a team player – the traits that will get you hired again and again.

Maintaining A Healthy Voice

Water, Water, Water

We all know we should drink our 6-8 glasses a day for good health, but good hydration is essential for great voices, too. This means, in part, singers should avoid too much caffeine, as it is a diuretic and will dehydrate their vocal cords. Caffeinated products to avoid include coffee, some teas, soft drinks and anything with chocolate *(bummer)*. Living in climates where forced air heat is prevalent can cause dehydration as well. Sugary beverages or dairy products a few hours prior to performing are not the greatest either as they may create a lot of phlegm in your throat...Ewwww!!!

Exercise

Is this starting to sound like a health magazine? I'm not preaching: I just want you to know that even moderate exercise can improve your breath control and phrasing immensely. Activities that are rhythmic in nature *(e.g., swimming, walking and running)* are extremely beneficial, as is anything that specifically concentrates on breathing, such as yoga.

Smoke, Smoke, Hack, Hack, Choke!

I know, I know – some of the greats were and are smokers. Well, some of them died from smoking, too. There are singers who claim to like the texture smoking gives their voice, but this habit will certainly diminish your breathing capacity. So, if you want to decrease your range, have less breath control and have more throat and sinus ailments, by all means, SMOKE!

Feeling Under The Weather

During cold and flu season, or if you fly frequently, there is always a fear that you will get sick and not be able to perform. Ironically, often the first place that gets affected is your voice. Rest is so important when you are coming down with something. I have also found great relief *(and even kept a throat ailment at bay)* by taking *Cold FX* or *oil of oregano* as soon as I feel the first throat tickle. I've never been a fan of throat-numbing drugstore remedies, as I am always afraid that after taking them, I'll unknowingly push my voice too hard and damage it. Instead, if a bug does take hold, visiting a steam room or holding your head over a facial steamer or bowl of hot water is very soothing and can give some relief.

If you do have to sing with a sore throat, you may find that you will need to be even more aware of your breathing rhythm, adding more breaths to stave off that *"needing to cough"* feeling. Hot water, lemon and honey is also a soothing drink to have on stage with you. For those of drinking age, sipping brandy or scotch *(don't tell my mom I said that)* can offer a bit of relief as well, but be discreet – don't get drunk and fall off the stage. *(LOL!)*

Laughing

There is no evidence that laughing is either voice-enhancing or detrimental, but I just recommend doing it 100 times or more a day because it feels so darn GOOD! Also, when navigating the shark-infested waters of the music business, you will need an exceptional sense of humour. I must attest, however, that the hundreds of times my *"sister from another mother" (Jake)* made me laugh on stage it was difficult to recover vocally – and the harder you laugh, the more the phlegm gets stirred up. Ewwww!!!

Your body, not only your voice is your instrument. Singing to your best ability will be easier if you try to keep the whole instrument in good shape and in good health.

Angela & Her "Sistah From Anotha Motha"
Jake Leiske
Photo by Lee Halliday

Glossary

air-to-tone ratio – the varying degrees of air released around the vocal tone originating from diaphragm support

"BG" – short form of "background" singer

backwards breathing – when taking in a breath of air the air tank *(or midsection/tummy)* pulls in instead of popping out

breathing rhythm – the pattern of breathmarks in the body of the song

breathmarks – the points in the song where you take a breath

chest breathers – people who breathe from the chest up not from the bellybutton up as singers should

chest voice/placement – the area of the body where your low notes resonate

diaphragm support – the surge of air created when the diaphragm is engaged to expel the air after taking in a singer's breath

dipthong – when one vowel has two vowel sounds *(e.g. "night" = Ni-eeght)*

Diva/Rockstar placement – the description of your notes when they are in your upper-mid range resonating just under your nose

Diva/Rockstar diaphragm support – the description of the substantial diaphragm support needed to keep your notes in diva/rockstar placement

floaty – an *"Angela word"* describing how a note should feel when it's effortless to sing

front of house – the place where the audience will be in front of the sound system

full voice/speaking tonality – the placement of your notes when they are in your mid-range in the vicinity of your chin or lower oral cavity

gear – equipment

"Grand Poobah" – the person who holds the highest rank in the situation

"H Seepage" – another *"Angela term"* describing the release of an "h" sound before a vowel thus wasting precious air support from the diaphragm

Heimlich Maneuver – a life saving exercise of pulling in a person's diaphragm from behind expelling what they may be choking on from the force of air created

high-range – the highest notes you can sing

low-range – the lowest notes you can sing

"mapping out" – marking breath marks, diaphragm support, trills, "colour words", vowel modifications etc. on a lyric sheet

Glossary

Mask Area Placement – the resonating area for your high range notes on either side of your nose

mic – short form of microphone

mid-range – the notes you sing just below the upper-mid-range notes and right above the low ones

oral cavity – the space in your mouth

phrase – the group of words between breathmarks

pitch – the accuracy of the note

power – the force created by engaging diaphragm support

range – all the notes you can sing from lowest to highest

residual air – the left over air in your "tank" at the end of a phrase

resonance – vibration or placement of a note

segue – a smooth transition from one thing to another

singer's breath – the movement of air in/tummy out from the bellybutton up

sound technician – a person who is skilled at running a sound system or studio equipment

squeezer – a singer who tightens their throat on the delivery of a note

stacking – when a singer adds a new breath on top of residual air

stage monitors – the equipment facing towards the stage or that are "in ear" in which vocals and instruments are heard through when performing

stylistic nuances – when vocal qualities such as tone, trills, diction, dynamics, rhythm etc. contribute to emotional value or to differentiate music styles

Supermask Placement – Mask Area Placement with intended Diva/Rockstar diaphragm support to create a bigger sound

tank – the midsection of the body from the bellybutton up

tone – the resonating sound of one's voice

tucker – a singer whose vocal path is too far back in their head

upper-mid-range – the notes that are just above the mid-range notes and just below the high-range notes

vocal mix – the balance of volumes between multiple singers

vocal path – the direction of sound a note travels once the diaphragm is engaged to support it

Notes

Notes

Notes

Notes

Photo by Lee Halliday. www.leehallidayphoto.com

Angela with her husband Doug & son Alex.

About The Author

Having graduated with honours from the Musician's Institute vocal program in Hollywood, California, Angela Kelman is known in music circles as one of the West Coast's premier vocal coaches.

"Learning good technique through proper breathing and placement of the voice is the secret to every singer's success." **This is Angela's mantra.** She has helped everyone from first time singers to recording artists who have needed a quick tune-up before going back into the studio. *"I have witnessed singers flourish with the smallest bit of knowledge. Everyone can be a better singer, it's just understanding how the voice works and remembering when and how to breathe."* Angela says.

After working as a professional singer in Winnipeg for seven years, Angela headed off to Hollywood, California to study at The Musician's Institute. "Studying at MI labelled a lot of things that I was already doing right technically and corrected the things that I was doing wrong. This enlightenment has ultimately preserved my voice and enabled me to develop my **5 Point Singing System.**" After MI, Angela travelled the world with her Juno and CCMA award winning group, **Farmer's Daughter** surviving a relentless tour schedule for many years with proper vocal technique.

Since the year 2000, Angela has been developing the **Five Point Singing System** to guide her students. She has shared this vocal technique with children and adults alike with amazing success.
"The greatest gift for me as a teacher is to help a student stay on pitch and sing with confidence and emotion, even if they were once self-described as a step away from being tone deaf."

"Singing is such an expression of one's heart and soul and is unique to each one of us. Let's face it, the reason we do it is because it feels so darn good." In using the **Five Point Singing System,** *Angela's greatest joy is helping people get over their fear to sing their heart out like no one is listening… and if someone is, this system will help* **"WOW"** *them.*

Currently, Angela lives in North Vancouver, BC Canada with her husband Doug and son, Alex. She teaches, writes children's sing-a-long books, records adult contemporary CDs, and performs with her dream band, The Polyester Philharmonic, continuing to be active in the Vancouver live performance and studio scene.

Acknowledgements

In creating this manual over the last two years I have enlisted the support, creativity and genius of many.

Thank you all from the bottom of my heart for helping to make my dream a reality.

Doug and Alex von Dersch

Jake Leiske

Gina Hole Lazarowich *(theyrep.com)*

Lee Halliday *(leehallidayphoto.com)*

Ken Stewart

Kim Norman, Shane Hendrickson *(shanehendrickson.com)*

Catherine St. Germain, Mike Reno *(loverboyband.com)*

Shaheed Khan *(khankreativ.ca)*

Claire Khan *(repart.com)*

Catherine Bowers

Elizabeth Wooding

Sue-Ann MacCara

Alyson Jones

Allan Rodger *(allanrodger.com)*

Sue and Steve Soucy

The Polyester Philharmonic

and all my wonderful students

Additional Products by Angela Kelman can be found at:

www.angelakelman.com

Café Brasilia

Café Brasilia/Casa Do Samba double CD set

www.singalongbooks.ca

Angela May's Magnificent Musical Menagerie – Juno Nominated Children's CD

Frank The Cat – Sing-Along Book

Disco Dinosaurs – Sing-Along Book

Funky Monkey – Sing-Along Book

www.5pointsingingsystem.com

5 Point Singing System Manual and Exercises

To access video tutorials visit **5pointsingingsystem.com/5pointvideos**

access code: **divas&rockstars**

Video Tutorials:

Singer's Breath

Diaphragm Support

Correct Placement For The Song

Microphone Technique

Placement / Resonance

Mapping Out Your Lyrics

Vocal Path

Vowel Modification

Troubleshooting Your Breathing

Warm Up Exercises 1 to 7

www.ingramcontent.com/pod-product-compliance
Lightning Source LLC
Chambersburg PA
CBHW041118300426
44112CB00002B/19